Kind Man, Strong Man

Men living without violence

Eric Hudson

First published by Busybird Publishing 2017

Copyright © 2017 Eric Hudson

ISBN
Print: 978-1-925692-27-3
Print: 978-1-925692-28-0

Eric Hudson has asserted his right under the Copyright, Designs and Patents Act 1988 to be identified as the author of this work. The information in this book is based on the author's experiences and opinions. The publisher specifically disclaims responsibility for any adverse consequences, which may result from use of the information contained herein. Permission to use information has been sought by the author. Any breaches will be rectified in further editions of the book.

All rights reserved. No part of this publication may be reproduced, stored in or introduced into a retrieval system, or transmitted in any form, or by any means (electronic, mechanical, photocopying, recording or otherwise) without the prior written permission of the author. Any person who does any unauthorised act in relation to this publication may be liable to criminal prosecution and civil claims for damages. Enquiries should be made through the publisher.

Cover design: Busybird Publishing

Layout and typesetting: Buybird Publsihing

Busybird Publishing
2/118 Para Road
Montmorency, Victoria
Australia 3094

www.busybird.com.au

This book is dedicated to all of the kind men, strong men I know who live their lives without violence. These are men who make sure that their partner and their children feel safe and are safe in their own homes, and in their relationships. These men live with respect and kindness. I think of men like David, Angus, Adam, Phil, Steve, Paul, Anthony, and many, many more.

Let's join them.

Contents

	Introduction	1
1	Setting the scene	7
2	Calling it what it is	11
3	Our focus is on men's violence	15
4	Men's violence takes many forms	21
5	You are still reading	27
6	What's it all about?	31
7	Stop thinking about causes	37
8	It's about control	43
9	More about control	47
10	Beliefs about being a man	53
11	Boys will be boys	57
12	Glass ceilings and other things	63
13	Male privilege	69
14	Masculinity and violence	77
15	Masculinity and sex	85
16	A summary: where have we explored so far?	91
17	Seeing another side to men	93
18	What goes on inside	101
19	The hidden emotion	105
20	Breaking the Cycle	113
21	On track	119
22	A path of courage	123
23	Facing up	127
24	What harm have I caused?	135
25	Repairing the harm	143
26	Safety, Safety, Safety	149
27	Watching our words	153
28	Re-building trust	161
29	Finding support	167
30	Raising your sons to be kind men, strong men	175
31	Staying in touch	181

Foreword

As a journalist, I first met Eric Hudson in the foyer of the Royal Commission into Institutional Responses to Child Sexual Abuse. Eric was providing emotional support to my friend Anthony Foster, whose daughters were raped by a priest.

The title of this book, Kind Man, Strong Man, is a perfect description of Anthony. The crimes against his family did not lead him to violence, rather he dedicated his life to a loving and caring campaign for justice. Anthony died earlier this year, leaving an outstanding legacy of courage, determination and change.

As a young footballer, I witnessed prolific men's violence and considered it normal. As a coach, years later, I learned these behaviours can be changed by striving to meet higher standards.

I read this book not as a journalist, footballer or coach. I read it as the son of a kind, strong, man, the father of three sons and a husband.

It made me want to be a better man. I think it will do the same for you.

I commend Eric on his leadership. And I thank him for being such a wonderful support to my beautiful mate Anthony, who is dearly missed.

Paul Kennedy
ABC News Breakfast

About the Author

Eric Hudson brings this conversation to you from many years of learning from men about their relationships.

He is a dad with four children and nine grandchildren.

He has been in professional roles where his participation has helped to promote kindness and safety in relationships. He has been particularly interested in supporting men in re-discovering their essential nature as kind, loving and safe participants in their own, and others' lives.

His work as a counsellor has also given him the privilege of listening to and learning from women who are living with the dilemma of loving the man in their lives but not wanting to continue to live with his violence. This work has also created the opportunity to listen to men and to talk with them about the changes they want to make in ending their violence, bringing safety and trust back to their families.

He has a deep understanding of the way that trauma plays out in people's lives. He understands the way that many vulnerable children who have been hurt by their father's violence, have gone on to be exposed to further violence and to be abused by others.

He firmly believes that violence is a choice and that it is possible for all men to live their lives without violence.

Introduction

You have just picked up this book and opened it.

For whatever reason, it has grabbed your attention.

I want to say to you:

"Now, right now, is the right time for you to be reading it."

I want us to think together about how we can be the men we really want to be in our homes and families.

Kind men.

Strong men.

As men, we often hit some big turning points in our lives.

Picking up this book and staying with it to the end may be the turning point that you have been looking for.

But you will need to stick with it.

This book is written to men, for men, by a man.

It is about how to do a better job in our families and how to do our bit to make them kind and safe places for everyone.

We all want to do the best that we can.

But we don't talk about this much.

I want you to imagine that you and I are sitting down somewhere together and having a chat about the things that really matter to us.

You might imagine any setting where you feel ok about having this talk together.

To be honest, it is a tough subject.

As men we have done a lot of harm in our homes and families, the places where we should all be the safest.

These are places where we should enjoy the most kindness in our lives, the most safety.

Being kind to one another in our families comes naturally.

When a new baby is born into a family, the natural response is to be loving and gentle and kind to that little one.

Children, by their nature, respond to kindness.

They respond with a natural delight.

Their innocent and natural joy is catching.

If you remember back to when your kids were born, you were filled with lots of hopes and dreams for them.

How is it then that violence finds a way into our families?

Why is it that violence is such a huge problem in our society?

Why is it that men's violence, in particular, is such an issue?

Men are the ones at the biggest risk of being hurt by violence.

But that risk comes from other men, mostly strangers, and in public places, outside of their homes.

Women are also at high risk of violence.

Though the risk of violence for women comes from their intimate male partners, and inside their own homes.

This is the place where they would expect to be the safest, and where they would expect to be treated the most kindly.

Violence towards others is a choice.

Men often choose the "when" of their violence.

They often choose the "where" and the "how" of their violence.

They also choose the "who" of their violence.

Violence is something we learn.

It is something children learn.

In particular, it is something we teach children, mostly our boys, as a part of being a "real man".

Road rage is an example of violence.

I sometimes wonder what difference it would make to safety on our roads if, every time we sat behind the wheel of a car or truck, or rode a motor bike or bicycle, we said to ourselves:

"Today, on the road, I am going to be safe.

I am going to think about how safely I drive or ride.

I am going to be kind to others on the road."

And then I wonder:

What would our homes and families be like if every man thought:

"Today I am going to be a safe dad. I will be kind today."

If every man held on to this idea.

If every man thought about it.

If every man acted on it.

As I have said already, I want you to experience this book as though we are having a simple, heart-to-heart talk together.

As though you and I are sitting down somewhere, talking about our homes and families, the people we love, and how we can do our bit to make sure that they are safe.

If you are serious about making a change in your family, you will need to keep going, keep on reading.

It may be difficult at times.

You may disagree with me at some points.

That is ok.

As long as we keep going on this journey of making our families safe places for everyone.

It would be good if this conversation makes a difference today for our families.

And it would be great if it made a difference for future generations.

It takes strength to have this conversation.

It takes guts.

Standing up.

Speaking up.

Facing up.

So that the ones we love, the women and children in our lives, feel safe, and are safe.

Will you join me in this conversation, as men, about men's violence?

This may be one of the most important conversations we could have together.

Thank you for joining me.

Your partner will thank you.

And so will your kids, and your grandkids.

ONE

Setting the scene

It is pretty clear that we have a big problem in this country.

And we have for a long time.

When I turn on the TV news there is often a story about yet another woman who has been killed or badly hurt by her boyfriend or husband or partner or her ex-partner.

Some people call this problem a national disaster.

It certainly seems like an epidemic.

What actually is the problem?

If we have a quick look at the statistics we start to get an idea of how big the problem is.

Even though this is not going to tell us the whole story, it is not a bad place to start.

The headlines tell us, "One woman in Australia is killed each week by her partner or ex-partner!" In fact it is actually higher than that.

Another statistic tells us that one out of every three women experiences violence from her partner or ex-partner at some point in her lifetime.

And we all know that there are heaps of women who never go to the police to report what happens to them.

How do we understand this issue that is called "domestic violence"?

This book will dig down into some of these issues so that we can talk about them more clearly.

There may be a few challenges in it.

There may be some points along the way where you start to think I have got it all wrong.

Let me ask you to just hang in there; don't give up on this conversation.

It is really important that we, as men, begin to think differently and act differently so that everyone is safe.

I have said already that this book is written for men to read and for men to talk about.

Women are welcome to read it too.

But remember, this is not women's problem to fix.

It is up to us, as men, to do something about it.

The starting point is to begin talking about this problem as something other than "domestic or family violence".

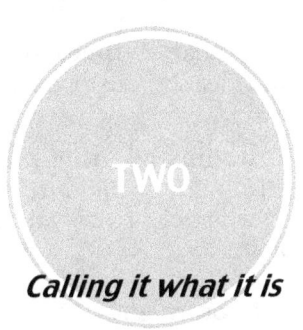

TWO

Calling it what it is

The terms "domestic violence" or "family violence" are sometimes swapped around to describe the same thing.

But they are not always helpful.

These terms tells us where the violence happens, in the home or family.

They may imply that responsibility for the violence is shared, that is, that both people in the relationship are responsible.

Using the term "domestic violence" keeps us caught in the idea that this is a relationship problem, and that both parties are part of the problem.

You have heard the old saying that "it takes two to tango"

That is what a lot of people think.

In fact, it is likely that at times you have caught yourself with this idea in your own mind.

Let me ask you to think of a time when you heard about a man getting angry and hitting his partner, and ask yourself whether or not you have begun to blame her in some way.

It is possible that you might have even thought or said something like, "yeah, but she would be absolute hell to live with!"

Or maybe something like:

"She is such a nag."

"She never shuts up."

"She is always on his back about something."

"Every man has his limits."

It is really easy to begin to think that the victim, the one who is hurt, is the one who is to blame.

It is important in this conversation that we keep a clear focus.

If we call it "domestic violence" it helps to keep the myth alive that women are the problem, that they are a part of the dynamic that causes men's violence, that somehow they bring it on themselves.

The term "domestic violence" is not a bad one necessarily, but it doesn't call it for what it is!

This book is about men's violence towards their partners.

This is the big issue.

This is what we need to do something about.

This is what I want us to talk about without being side-tracked.

It is too easy to shift our focus away from this one issue of men's violence to blame their girlfriends, their wives, their partners, their ex-partners.

So, from here on, we will stop using the terms "domestic violence" or "family violence".

We will start talking about **men's violence.**

We will call it what it is.

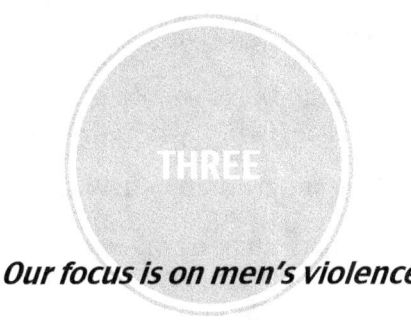

THREE

Our focus is on men's violence

If we want to get anywhere in doing something about this huge problem in our country we need to face the issues squarely.

If we want to protect women and children in their own homes, we have to begin by calling this violence what it actually is: men's violence toward their intimate female partners.

You might already be reacting and disagreeing with me.

That's ok, because there's a lot to work out and talk about.

Don't give up just because you have a different idea.

Let's start by talking about some ideas that often crop up.

Mostly I hear two common objections to focussing on men's violence:

Not all men are violent, so why call it men's violence?

Women are violent too, or women are just as violent as men. Let's take a look at these objections.

There may be some truth in both of them.

However, they both steer us off course, they get us off-track.

They shift our focus away from thinking about the main issue, that is, doing something about the way that men hurt their intimate female partners.

Imagine how our society would be different if we could do something to end men's violence against women, if we could do something to change just this one issue.

Imagine if, as a society we could do something to ensure that women and children are safe in their own homes.

Imagine.

If we could keep our focus on this one issue and not get off-track, we might be able to begin to make some real changes.

Let's look a bit more closely at the first objection that "not all men are violent".

It is absolutely true that the majority of men are not violent to their partners.

The majority of men are loving, caring, affectionate, supportive, hard working, sacrificial, SAFE men.

Kind men. Strong men.

I whole-heartedly believe this.

We can celebrate this reality, and we can acknowledge it and be grateful to those men in our lives who are safe husbands, partners, fathers, sons, brothers, friends.

It is true, not all men are violent.

But if we want to address the big issue of men's violence, it will not help if we water it down by saying "it's not all men".

However, we only need to look at the statistics to know how much damage and hurt is caused by some men against their intimate female partners.

The overwhelming majority of violence against women is inflicted by the men in their lives.

If we can begin to talk about this violence as men's violence, then we can talk about it squarely for what it is.

And we can begin to do something about it.

And, there is a deeper, stronger challenge for all men.

The challenge is to see that men's violence begins in all of our attitudes and values towards women.

All men, whether we are violent to our intimate partners or not, may hold some attitudes and values that contribute to a society in which women are not respected or treated as equals.

Now to the second objection that "women are violent too".

I can honestly say that every time I speak somewhere about men's violence, somebody will come up with the objection that it's not just men, that women are violent too.

Notice how this objection has immediately shifted our focus.

Our attention has gone to something else.

We have started to let the men who use violence off the hook.

It reminds me of kids at school caught out for doing something wrong, and they reply with, "It's not just me, he started it!"

The issue of women's violence towards men is an old argument that does not get us anywhere, especially if we want to do something to end men's violence.

Nor does it stand up against the evidence.

What I am wondering about is what purpose it serves to raise this objection.

I am wondering if it is another way of blaming women for men's actions.

I am wondering if it is a way of making someone else responsible.

What I want us to keep our focus on is men's violence against women because that is the really big issue that we need to do something about.

That is what this book is about: men's violence against their intimate female partners.

This is where we need to keep our focus.

This is what we need to change.

FOUR

Men's violence takes many forms

I remember so clearly the moment when a woman said to me, "You know, he has never hit me, never laid a hand on me, but there are sometimes when I wish he would hit me! Because then I would have the bruises on the outside where they can be seen, not on the inside where no-one can see them."

This woman was a very well-dressed, well-groomed, well-educated, professional woman.

Her husband was what could be described as a "pillar of society".

He too was a well-educated professional, church-going man, respected in his community.

But behind closed doors he was a tyrant of abuse.

His wife was bruised and battered, on the inside.

Not by physical beatings to her body but by the put downs, humiliations, name calling, rules, orders, demands, controls on what she could eat or clothes she could buy, limits on her friendships, and demands for sex.

What I understood really clearly the day I listened to her was that men's violence takes many forms.

They are all abusive behaviours, even without actual physical violence, and they add up to what I am talking about when I use the term "men's violence".

I am also reminded of the many times I have heard men say to me, "You know, I have never actually hit her!"

What an interesting thing to tell me.

One of the things I hear in that statement is that he perhaps holds the belief that this would actually be the wrong thing for him to do.

He is telling me something about the values he holds.

"It is not right to hit a woman or a girl" is a commonly held idea that many men and boys grow up with.

The other thing I hear in this statement is that there may have been times when he has actually thought about hitting her, or has maybe threatened to hit her, or has maybe even been really close to hitting her and been very intimidating.

Another possibility is that he knows he has many other ways to keep her doing what he wants, so that he doesn't have to hit her.

So the statement "I have never actually hit her" holds a number of possible meanings.

One of the main things that most women who experience violence know is that men's violence may take many forms.

A man's violence is normally a mix of a whole lot of different behaviours that he uses.

And they are sometimes really subtle, hardly seen or known about, and easily excused with words like "I was just trying to help you".

These subtle behaviours are really tricky because they are so easy to deny.

And they are easy to play down by saying, "it wasn't that bad" or "that's not what I did".

These sneaky, tricky, "undercover", but very intentional, behaviours are also really easy to blame on the other person by suggesting that the other person is too sensitive, or needs to toughen up.

My point is that men's violence is not just about physical violence.

What we are talking about is the whole bag of controlling and abusive behaviours that a man might use, behaviours that are directed towards controlling, or undermining, or intimidating, or punishing, or making her do what he wants.

I clearly remember the time when a woman apologised because she could not afford to pay for her counselling session.

We talked about this some more.

She was able to tell me that her husband had a good full time job and was well paid. He controlled all of the family finances. He did all of the grocery shopping and paid all of the bills. He had accumulated quite a reasonable amount of savings in an account in his name. The only money that she had was the family allowance that was paid into a bank account in her name. She used this money for all of the kid's birthday and Christmas presents and for any of her own clothes. She also used it to pay for counselling.

As we talked that day I understood about his financial control. And she was also able to tell me that there were times when he would tell her off for her mistakes, that he would bully her, and even that he would hit her.

This was a very important conversation because it allowed her to take the brave step of telling someone else about the ways that he controlled and abused her and used physical violence against her.

In this conversation that you and I are now having together, it will be important to remember that men's violence is made up of many different types of actions and behaviours, that it is much more than hitting and pushing.

You may be reading this and thinking that your violence and abuse isn't a problem anymore because you have separated.

It is important to recognise that a man's violence, abuse and control towards his partner will most likely continue, and even get worse, even after that relationship has ended.

Separation is one of the most dangerous times for women in a relationship. The risk of physical violence gets worse.

And, even though they are no longer living together, the opportunities for verbal and emotional abuse are not lessened.

If his partner ended the relationship, then ongoing blame, put downs, criticism and arguments (mostly about the children) are likely to continue and are all very common.

You are still reading

Here you are at the fifth chapter, and you are still with me!

I want to ask you to take a break and think about something.

I would like you to consider what it says about you that you are still giving this book a go, that you have stuck at it so far for four chapters.

There have been some challenging ideas so far.

Maybe even ideas you want to argue about or disagree with.

So, what does this say about you?

There are several possible answers.

The first that comes to my mind is that you are

taking this subject seriously.

The second is that perhaps you want to help to make a difference.

Making a difference might mean taking a good look at our own beliefs and behaviours.

A third thing that this might say about you, is that, as a man, you have some strong reactions to the idea that women and children are not safe in their own homes, in the one place in their lives where they should be the safest.

Or perhaps you hold some feelings of regret about some of your own past actions, where you have hurt the ones you love.

And there may be a bigger picture.

As a man in our society you may want to do more to help to stop men's violence against women and children.

You may feel bad that you have been silent and have not taken a stand against other men's violence against women and children.

If we really want to do something to end men's violence, there are some really big issues for us as men to face.

So I invite you to stay with me.

Please feel free to disagree with me.

I may not be right about everything but it is good for us all to think about this very important issue and to try to sort it out so that we can all take action to stop it.

What's it all about?

Let's turn our thoughts now to the question of what we think men's violence is all about.

Let's see if we can get our heads around it.

You probably have a few ideas about this already.

Sometimes the ideas that we hold about what the problem is will influence the solutions that we come up with.

When I was a teenager and I was mowing the lawn and the mower would break down, I used to think it was the dirty spark plug that was the problem. So I would take the spark plug out and clean it the best I could, put it back in and try again, and off we would go.

For a while!

Until it stopped again.

And then I would go through the whole thing again,

over and over again. Frustrating.

I wasn't getting to the real problem.

We often like to think about what causes a problem.

If we can work that out, we can come up with a solution.

Trying to get our heads around the problem of men's violence against women is important because if we do not understand it clearly, we will keep going round in circles.

Nothing will change and women and children will remain at risk.

When we think about what causes men's violence, we normally come up with some ideas pretty quickly.

One of the most common ideas is that men's violence is caused by drug and alcohol abuse.

It is certainly true that drug and alcohol abuse is often involved in incidents of violence.

It is often referred to as "alcohol or drug related violence".

Sure, drinking too much doesn't help.

But whether we can say that it causes men's violence is questionable.

There can be different reactions to situations when

someone has had too much to drink, or when someone has been using drugs.

Let's think about a typical relationship situation:

A couple are at a party and the guy has too much to drink with his mates.

He starts to behave badly, and his partner suggests it's time to go home.

He does not want to go home yet.

She goes away and comes back a bit later and asks him again.

He tells her to leave him alone and get off his back.

It's getting late and she tries a third time.

But this time he is ready to go.

They leave, and she drives.

In the car, he starts on at her.

Things like how dare she get on his case in front of his mates.

What did she think she was doing?

Doesn't she trust him to know when he has had enough to drink?

One day she had better learn how to treat him properly.

She drives in silence.

She expected that this would happen after he had been drinking so much.

She also knew that he would want to have sex when they got home.

The last thing that she wanted was for him to force himself on her, get what he wanted and then leave her feeling used and abused.

This is exactly what happened though.

And more!

Not only did he rape her (that is, force her to have sex against her will, without her consent,) but he also roughed her up a bit, so that the next day she had bruises appearing on her body.

Not where anyone could see them though.

It would be easy to conclude from this story, that his violence was caused by his drinking.

It was definitely fuelled by the fact that he was drunk!

And it was worse than normal.

But what we know about this man's violence towards his partner is that he behaves this way towards her even when he has not been drinking.

He treats her this way when he hasn't been drinking at all.

And, when he was drunk at the party he did not choose to bash anyone else.

This man is never violent towards his mates when he is drunk.

If he has had too much to drink, why is it that the alcohol does not cause him to be violent to them.

How come he only targets his partner?

This is the reality.

She is the target of his violence and abuse when he has been drinking and when he has **not** been drinking.

Sure, it's worse when he is drinking, but it is not the only time when she is frightened of him.

The fact is that she lives in fear of his violence most of the time.

She never knows when he will blow up or what will set him off, whether he has been drinking or not.

The point is that his abusive and violent behaviours form a part of an overall pattern of control of his partner, which leaves her living in fear.

The idea that his violence is caused by his abuse of alcohol is unhelpful.

In a way it excuses his violence, and shifts the focus to "if only we can get him to stop drinking".

Helping a man to stop his drinking as a way of ending his violence will not be enough.

There is no doubt that this may be good for his general health and well-being.

It might change some of his alcohol fuelled violence.

But fundamentally it will not change any of his other behaviours or attitudes.

It is important to add though that if you know that your life is seriously affected and your life choices are limited by your use of alcohol and other drugs, then you might give strong consideration to seeking help from a professional.

Start by talking to your GP.

SEVEN

Stop thinking about causes

It is quite natural to think about what causes a problem.

If only we knew what causes it, we could fix it!

There are many commonly held ideas about what causes men's violence, similar to the idea that alcohol abuse causes men's violence.

We could spend a lot of time thinking about them and testing them, but we would come up with the same idea:

- the explanations don't really work
- they are excuses
- they shift the responsibility
- they don't go to the heart of the issue
- they don't lead us to real change.

Some of the common things that are thought to cause men's violence are things like:

- He is depressed, he is anxious, he is not well

- He is stressed or overworked

- He has a short fuse. He cannot control his temper

- He grew up with a violent father. He learnt it from his dad

- It's a part of his culture. (Show me any culture where men's violence against women is not a problem!)

You will have heard all of these things before.

But none of them really work as explanations.

For example, why is it that some men who have grown up in what we commonly call a "white Anglo or western culture" are never violent to their partners, and many are?

Can we blame their culture?

If we stopped thinking about what causes men's violence, then how do we get our heads around it?

It would be good if we could struggle honestly with this big question of what men's violence is all about.

Let's just go back to the discussion about alcohol for a little while.

The question that is in my head is:

"Why is it that some men who drink too much would never think about hitting or hurting their partners, while other men, when they have too much to drink, their partner is the first and only person they hurt?"

This may be a helpful question to think about.

If we could really understand the differences we might start to understand that the issue is not his drinking.

It is something else.

It may be helpful to think about how the men who hurt their partners behave when they have **not** been drinking.

We have talked about this already and know the answer.

His partner is afraid of him most of the time, drinking or not drinking.

Another question we could ask is:

"Have men who have stopped drinking completely, also stopped their violence against their female partners?"

Tricky question!

It is very likely that they have stopped or changed

some things, but their abusive behaviours are still going on.

They are very likely still doing the other things that control, undermine, put down and intimidate their partners, perhaps with reduced physical violence or none at all.

Remember, when we are talking about men's violence against women, we are not only talking about their physical violence.

We are talking about a range of other abusive and controlling behaviours including verbal abuse, mental and emotional abuse, spiritual abuse, financial abuse, sexual abuse.

So what is different?

When they are drunk, some men are violent and abusive.

Other men when they are drunk wouldn't hurt a fly.

Let's think about another really familiar idea about what causes men's violence.

I will call it "the short fuse" explanation.

This is the idea that some men just have bad tempers.

They explode really quickly.

It is a part of their nature, they were born with it.

Sometimes people think that it is because his own father got angry easily, "He is just like his dad. If only he could learn to control his anger."

A man's violence is often seen as being caused by his inability to control his anger.

In truth, he has very good control of his anger.

He knows when to turn it on, and when to turn it off.

He makes clear choices about who to be angry with, and who not to be angry with.

He also makes choices about where to be angry, and where not to be angry.

Even after completing an "anger management program" where he has learnt some useful anger control strategies, it is very likely that the range of his abusive and violent behaviours towards his intimate female partner will continue.

Like drinking, and anger, there are many ideas about what causes men's violence.

We could actually say the same thing about all of these explanations.

They are mostly excuses, they don't work, they don't fit, they take us off-track, they do not lead to real change.

In short, it is not helpful to try to sort this issue out by thinking about what causes men's violence.

But if we stop asking about causes, what else might help us to understand the problem?

EIGHT

It's about control

A helpful way to think about these issues is to listen to some men themselves.

It has been a while now since I began to work in group programs with men who wanted to stop their violence against their intimate female partners.

Listening to these men was a good way for me to understand more about men's violence.

- These were ordinary blokes.
- From every walk of life.
- From every family background.
- From every social background.
- They were in the group by their own choice.

All of the stereotypes about men who use violence disappeared for me as I met each man and heard about his use of violence.

What did these men help me to understand?

I remember the very first group. I shared the leading of the group with a female colleague.

It was her first group of this type too.

I had done a lot of reading, training and learning about men's violence.

But I still remember being shocked at the things that the men told us.

I remember reading how some men harm their partners' pets as a way of controlling and intimidating them.

I remember my shock when I heard men tell the group that they had actually done this.

What I realised was that when a man harms a pet, it is a warning to his partner that he can hurt her in the same way.

By listening to all of the men in these groups, I began to understand the many tactics that men use to deliberately intimidate, threaten and control their partners.

It might be useful for you to make your own list of the things that you have heard from other men or even better, from the things that you have done yourself, that have been deliberately aimed at controlling your partner.

Making a list like this may be helpful in looking closely at your own actions and getting a clear picture of all of the things you do that hurt others.

It may be useful to buy a notebook that you can use to write down your thoughts and ideas, or to keep track of your own progress.

Knowing about all of the tactics that men use to control their partners helps to keep us more aware of our own behaviours.

Making a list also helps to see and understand our own patterns more clearly.

The pattern that I have heard from men is basically about control.

This is what it generally boils down to.

When men begin to talk about the things they have done to their partners it comes down to getting them to do what they want, or stopping them from doing something they don't like.

Control is the common theme.

Alcohol, drugs, stress, depression, anxiety, anger, culture, family background all may be a part of the story.

But not always.

They are not consistently present in the lives of all men who use violence.

There is, however, one consistent theme that men talk about and that theme is about wanting to control their partners in some way.

NINE

More about control

Let's use an example.

We will talk about Ron.

He's been telling me about some of his physical violence towards Liz.

(Apologies to any Ron or Liz reading this.)

He has been describing the way he loses his temper and slams his fists on the table, pushes his chair back from the table, storms out of the room and shoves Liz, knocking her from her chair as he goes.

I asked Ron to tell me about this incident.

He told me that Liz asked him if he had paid the electricity bill.

He was beginning to blame her and make it her fault.

He then described how she didn't give up.

Over dinner, she asked him three times.

He had forgotten to pay the bill but did not want to say so.

"I just wanted her to shut up!"

Ron had a reliable way of getting what he wanted, of getting his partner to do what he said.

In this case, what he wanted was for her to shut up.

He wanted her to stop asking him questions.

In short, Ron's actions, his violence and abuse, were aimed at control: getting Liz to do what he wanted and when he wanted.

This may be a difficult idea to swallow.

I don't think any person really likes the idea that their actions are intended to control another person, especially if that person is their partner.

I think it is tough for a man to own up to this.

It is easier to say, "I've just got a short fuse. My dad had a short fuse too."

As we keep going through this book and working our way through these issues, I ask you to keep this idea in mind: men's violence is basically about control.

Even if you don't agree with me, simply hold this idea as a possibility.

We need to understand more about this.

As you do, it will help you to let go of ideas that excuse him, or that blame his partner, or do not help us to find ways to stop his violence.

I invite you to think about other stories you have heard from men about their violence.

Or if you are up for it, to think about your own acts of violence or control.

Some useful questions to ask are:

- What did you do?
- What did you want to happen by your use of violence or abuse?

Asking yourself these questions is a good way to get to the bottom of things.

It might be helpful for you to write some things down in your notebook.

Think about a recent incident where you have done something that you have not been happy about.

It might be a similar situation to the one with Ron and Liz described above.

Or it could be completely different.

Put yourself under the microscope.

Have a close look and be honest with yourself: what did you do, what did you say, how did you say it?

Then ask yourself what did you want to achieve by doing it?

Back to Ron's example.

Asking him: "What did you do?"

He might say: "I hit the table, pushed my chair over, and shoved Liz."

(Notice that this is not the full story about what he did. Liz would have a more complete version of events if she were telling the story.)

"What did you want to happen?"

"I wanted her to shut up about the electricity bill."

This is an important step for Ron in working out what he wanted Liz to do.

The next thing to get to the bottom of is Ron's beliefs, the ideas he has in his head.

A good way to get an idea of this is to start a sentence with the words "She should have …"

What do you think Ron would say?

It might be something like this:

"She should know not to hassle me. She should know to shut up when I tell her to."

These words tell us something about what Ron believes.

Ron doesn't think that Liz should hassle him.

It is not her place to do this.

She should also do what he says.

He thinks it is ok for him to tell Liz what to do.

Ron thinks he should be the one in charge.

Does this make sense to you?

The idea I am getting at is that most, if not all of what we do, is built on our underlying beliefs.

All of our actions are supported or motivated by underlying beliefs that we hold.

What we do, what we say, how we act, all of it, has its foundations in the ideas, beliefs, and values that we hold.

The beliefs that we hold are the engine room that drives our actions.

When it comes to the issue of men's violence towards their intimate female partners, this all gets boiled down to some basic beliefs that some men hold about themselves, and their rights and their power as men.

In addition, there are some underlying beliefs they hold about women.

As you read this, notice what you are saying to yourself.

Is this making sense to you?

Are you arguing in your mind with me?

If so, I want to ask you to hang in there with me.

Keep on going.

This is an important point to be clear about.

I am clear about this because it is what I have heard from men when they have been talking with me about their violence.

Beliefs about being a man

One of the tough things in talking to men about their violence, is to ask them to describe what they have actually done that hurts or harms their partners in some way.

This is a big step for a man in facing squarely what he has done.

What a tough thing to do!

When I am having a conversation with a man about his violence, one of the things that I ask him to do is to imagine that we are sitting together watching the CCTV footage of an incident where he is being violent towards his partner.

I ask him to focus on what he is saying or doing on the screen.

And I then ask him to describe his own behaviours and actions to me.

This is normally very challenging and confronting.

To gain at least some idea of how difficult this may be, recall the last time that you were pulled over by the police.

Bring to mind the way that you "umm'd and ahh'd" as you were asked to explain why you might have been pulled over.

It was probably very difficult to say that you were using your phone and did not see the red light.

For a man to describe honestly his violent actions towards his partner is a difficult thing to do.

He will probably never get the whole truth out.

But having an honest go at it is a brave thing to do.

Listening to men themselves describe their actions towards their partners is very interesting.

Men's violence is mostly directed towards a specific goal or outcome.

This can most simply be described as "getting her to do something that he wants her to do!"

In other words, to control her.

Remember, these are not my ideas, or ideas I found in a textbook.

This is what I have heard from men themselves.

And they often tell me more.

Sometimes men begin to open up and talk about their underlying ideas that fuel their actions and their goals.

Let's go back to Ron for a while.

What other ideas or beliefs do you think Ron holds that might fuel his actions described above?

What is Ron thinking?

What do you think Ron would say?

Perhaps it is something like this:

"What right does she have to go on about the electricity bill?"

"Who does she think she is?"

"She should shut up when I tell her to."

"I earn the money, I pay the bills, what business is it of hers?"

"This is my house, she should be quiet when I say so."

"She is always on my back, always at me, nagging me."

Any one of these ideas is possible.

What is common to them?

They basically all come down to ideas that Ron holds about himself and his position in his family.

Ron believes that he is the one who is in charge.

It is his right to be in charge.

He is the boss.

Old fashioned stereotypes you might say.

They might remind you of ideas you heard from your father or grandfather, but that you think are no longer common.

I invite you to watch and listen and notice how commonly these ideas might still be held by men.

When we think about men's violence as an issue of men's belief in their right to be in control, their right to be in charge, to be the boss, then we can start to think about the **context** of men's violence, not the causes.

It actually begins to lead us in a productive direction towards change.

Some of this change can begin as we raise our children differently, teaching values of respect, equality and non-violence.

ELEVEN

Boys will be boys

What do I mean by the context of men's violence?

A simple story to share.

I know, in some ways it is quite harmless.

But I was a bit shocked by it.

I was at the beach.

This year.

There were some families nearby with four or five kids between them, a mix of boys and girls.

As they were leaving one of the dads was chanting with the boys:

"Boys are the best!

Girls are the worst!

Boys are the best!

Girls are the worst!"

Of course the boys joined in the chant.

They were having fun together. Harmless enough. No big deal.

But it helps to show what I mean by "context".

By context I mean the mix of ideas and beliefs that exist in a society, the ideas and beliefs that we grow up with, that we hear from other people.

We take them on board.

We make them our own and we pass them on in what we say and what we do.

We act out these ideas, values, beliefs.

When we are thinking about the context of men's violence, we are thinking about all of the ideas, values and beliefs that fuel, support or motivate men's violence.

These ideas help to form behaviours that are repeated and become patterns.

These ideas are sometimes passed from one generation to the next.

In this way they develop a sense of certainty.

This is how things are or how things are meant to be.

It's almost as though there is some order or rule or law of nature.

We accept it without question.

What ideas or beliefs might men hold that support men's violence?

When we come to this question we have very, very deep foundations that have formed over hundreds of years.

These ideas and beliefs are in the "very air that we breathe".

As one man said to me, "I feel like I have been marinated in them!"

As an example of these ideas, when did you last hear someone say, "boys will be boys"?

This is a simple idea or belief about males that is just one small part of what I mean by the **context** of men's violence.

"Boys will be boys."

When do we hear this?

It is sometimes used to refer to children, little boys mucking around, playing, getting a bit energetic or wild, or even beginning to rumble or fight.

It seems strange that we do not have a similar saying, "girls will be girls", that we use when girls start to get a bit wild or start rumbling with each other.

I have also heard this saying used about older boys, teenagers, or even adult men.

About men of all ages in fact.

Mostly it is used when males of any age are mucking around, "behaving badly", rumbling, fighting, getting drunk. In general, it is used when they are thought to be doing something "bad" or "wrong".

It is used as an excuse.

"Oh well, don't worry about it. They are boys. They are just doing what comes naturally. Boys will be boys."

"Doing what comes naturally."

Often, being violent is thought about as a natural way for men to be, as though it is a part of their very make-up.

The result is that disrespectful, abusive and violent actions are excused.

Men are let off the hook.

They are excused because "they are just doing what comes naturally".

I wonder if there are other ideas like this one that might in some way be a part of a group of ideas or beliefs that are all similar and that have a similar impact.

What other ideas might help to build up a picture of the way that men should be, that support the idea that it is ok and only natural for men to be violent?

It is this group of ideas, or beliefs, or values that are commonly held in our society, and the patterns and practices that have developed as a result, that I address when I talk about the context of men's violence.

How do we fully understand this idea of the **context** of men's violence?

How has this context developed over time?

How is it maintained?

My invitation to you at this point is to begin making a list of all of the things that you know about, all of the examples that you can think of, that in some way encourage a belief that it is normal and natural for men to be "in charge" over women.

For men to be in control.

And for men to use violence as a way of maintaining that control.

I invite you to observe and notice some of the ideas, values and beliefs that exist in our society.

They have existed for a very long period of time.

Some of these ideas are not just about men, but they are also ideas and beliefs about women. Some have their roots in history but still affect us today.

It is not long ago that women did not have the right to vote or to stand for election to government.

It is also not that long ago that married women did not generally work in paid employment outside of the home.

The norm was for wives and mothers to be at home, cooking, cleaning, and looking after the kids.

Women were called "housewives".

A lot has changed since then.

But it also seems that many of the typical ideas about men and women, and the natural order of things, still hang around.

I am wondering about other "old ideas" that might be still hanging around.

"A woman's place is in the home."

"It's a man's world."

"Don't be such a girl", carries the implication that there is something wrong or less about being a girl.

"This job needs a real man", indicating that there is a fixed idea about what a real man is, and that there are certain tasks that belong only to men, that women cannot or should not do.

TWELVE

Glass ceilings and other things

As well as thinking about these ideas, it is worth thinking about some of the structures in our society that may also contribute to the context of men's violence.

There are some stand-out themes.

Think about government.

How many women are there in our parliaments? In Cabinets? As Prime Ministers or Premiers?

Is it surprising that political parties need to establish quotas for the number of women who will be selected as candidates for upcoming elections?

Women's right to vote, that we have just talked about. What do the history books tell us about this, about when women were seen as having the same rights as men to participate in the democratic system of government, by having the right to vote? Is it still history making to have a female President, Prime Minister, or head of government?

If we go to the business sector and ask about the number of CEOs of large corporations who are women, or who serve as board members or directors, we find a similar history of domination in these roles by men.

The "glass ceiling" is a term that has been used for many years to describe the barriers that exist for women climbing the ladder of corporate leadership.

It still exists.

In the religious sphere we could consider the long battle that women have had to find positions of leadership and recognition for their abilities in these institutional structures.

The ordination of women (official recognition of women to hold positions of leadership and to conduct services) is still hotly contested in many religious organizations.

In the sporting world, it is rare for the achievements of women to receive the same media attention as men. In a country where sport is so highly valued and promoted there is a huge difference in the value and promotion of women's sport. Sponsorship support flows readily to male sporting codes but a much smaller bucket of money is available for female codes. Sponsorship deals are hard won by female athletes and prize money, where available, is often a much lower amount.

It is refreshing to see a TV news sports segment begin with and highlighting the sporting achievements of women before it moves to the coverage of a male sporting team.

In government, business, religion and sport we see clear examples of the power, importance and position of men.

And when we think of many of our family traditions and customs, it is not difficult to find examples that have their roots deep in history and are clear statements about the place of men and women.

When we celebrate the announcement of an upcoming wedding, or when we participate in a family wedding, we see clear evidence of these beliefs.

An engagement ring worn by the bride-to-be, is an age old tradition signifying betrothal.

It basically indicates that she is promised to another man, she is "taken".

Wedding rings, at least in some traditions, were a symbol of ownership, a way for the man to claim his wife.

In the wedding ceremonies that I have attended over time, it is normally the father of the bride who "gives her away" to the new man in her life ("Who gives this woman to be married to this man?" as the father passes his daughter's hand across to the groom.)

All of these customs reflect a time when wives were thought of as the "property" of their husbands.

In some wedding ceremonies there was a time when the bride would even promise to obey her husband.

The same promise was not required of the husband.

When I was a kid, my mother would receive letters addressed to her as "Mrs...", followed by my father's full name, not her own name.

Here we have another example of a cultural tradition that was so widely held that it seemed normal or natural, it was just how things were.

The titles, "Mrs" and "Miss" indicated a woman's relationship to a man, whether married to a man, or not.

Whereas men have only one title, "Mr" which does not indicate anything about his relationship to a woman.

When my Mum and Dad were married in the 1940s it was just assumed that women would take their husband's name. This had been a long historical and cultural practice.

Fifty years later though, if a couple marry, it is more likely for the woman to maintain her birth name.

Many of these practices and customs have been changing over time.

When we look closely at many of them they have a link back to fixed ideas of the superiority of men over women, the natural right of men to be leaders, for men to be the "head" of the house, for men to be decision makers and to have control.

However, while many of our customs and practices are changing, the ideas, beliefs and values that established these customs have not changed very much.

They all contribute to the context for men's violence against women.

I am asking you to think about the issue of men's violence a bit differently to how we commonly think about a problem.

Mostly we want to think about what causes a problem.

This way we can find a way of fixing it.

Instead of thinking about the causes of men's violence it may be more helpful to make a shift and to think about the context of men's violence.

This will mean taking a good hard look at many aspects of our society, our cultures and traditions, our organisations, our media, in fact everything that contributes to the ideas, beliefs and values that men hold that may support their use of violence.

THIRTEEN

Male privilege

It will be useful to think together a little more about this idea of the beliefs and values that help to build the context for men's violence.

To do this I want to return to some of the conversations that men have with me about their violence.

As we start this part of our conversation it is helpful to remember how difficult it is for most human beings to face up and to speak up about our actions, especially when and if we have hurt other people.

I sometimes use the "fly on the wall" image. This is a little bit like the CCTV image that I talked about earlier:

"Just imagine for a moment if I were a fly on the wall during that argument, and I could see and hear what was happening. I am interested to know the things I would I see you doing, or the things I would I hear you saying."

This is a supportive, but direct way for a man to begin to take an objective look at his own actions, and to begin describing them.

As I have said before, it takes some guts for a man to honestly fess up to what he has done.

After the man has described what he has done, and given me a fairly honest account of his actions, I then want to know about his intentions: what it was that he wanted to happen by doing this?

If you think back to the earlier example of Ron and Liz, in Ron's words, he "just wanted Liz to shut up!" Ron is pretty straight forward about what he wants.

Most of the men I have talked to say something like this:

Their actions are aimed at getting their partners to do something that they want them to do: shut up, get out of my way, get me this or that, slow down, get off my back.

And then I wonder about the beliefs that are underneath what he has done, and what he wants. It seems clear to me that there is a strong belief system that supports these actions and intentions.

I want to know about the underlying beliefs that a man has that support his violent actions towards his partner.

Let's go back to Ron for a bit.

"I would like to understand a bit more Ron. You have told me that you shoved and hit Liz. You wanted her to shut up and get off your back. I am interested in what else you were thinking to yourself."

What do you think Ron might say?

It is possible that Ron might be thinking something like:

"Just do as I say Liz, leave me alone."

Or

"Do as you are told. I have told you once. Drop it!"

Or he might be thinking something even stronger:

"Why can't she just shut up, leave it to me, and get off my case. I am the man here. I'm in charge."

There may be other thoughts that you have about what Ron might have been thinking.

When men are asked to explore and dig down into their own beliefs, they mostly get to some idea about them being the one in charge.

It might be difficult to get your head around what I am saying here.

But I have heard this often from men.

This underlying pattern of beliefs is so familiar for men when they are talking about their use of violence.

The pattern is very clear.

The underlying beliefs are about what they see to be "the natural right of men to have power over women, for men to be in charge, the ones in control".

It is a deep down belief in the superiority of men over women.

It is a belief that there is a natural order of life.

In this natural order of life, men are believed to be stronger and more powerful than women.

The belief establishes that men have a right to have power over women.

For some men, being in charge means using whatever force or power they have to ensure compliance with their wishes.

When young men are asked about their relationships with the opposite sex,

what becomes obvious is that they often hold strong ideas about their rights as males.

This is especially so when it comes to having sex.

Many believe that if they take a girl out and pay for her meal or the movies, that they could rightly expect to have sex with her at the end of the night.

They also believe that if they start to make out, to get aroused, that the girl has to see it through; she wouldn't be able to say no and stop.

When surveys are completed about men's ideas it

is not uncommon to find that many ideas about the superiority of men still persist.

Even though the world is changing and in some parts of society men and women are thought to be equal, there seem to be many men who still hold onto strong ideas about being the boss, the one in charge, the leader, more important or superior to the women in their lives.

They know best.

Their decisions are better.

They are the ones who make the big decisions.

Let's go back to Ron and Liz again for a bit.

Ron has told me that he hit and shoved Liz because he wanted her to shut up and get off his back. And when we talked a little about the beliefs underneath this he said: "Well, she should know to shut up when I tell her to."

That little word "should" is a real clue that Ron is getting down to talking about his beliefs.

What else do you think Ron might say if he goes a bit further?

It might be something like this:

"Well Liz knows what I am like. She knows that I like things done my way. She should know when I am starting to get angry. She should back off when I tell her to. This is my house."

Ron seems to hold some strong ideas about his place in his family.

He hasn't quite said it, but it's quite clear that Ron thinks he is the one who is in charge and that Liz should do what he says and when he says it.

I sometimes wonder what it would be like if we lived in a world where men and women were given equal respect, equal rights, and were equally valued for their unique personal contributions within their families.

I wonder if a man valued and respected his partner as his equal in this way, whether he would ever act violently or abusively towards her.

The idea of "male privilege" is often rejected as nonsense, especially by some men.

But if we open our eyes and ears to it, and especially begin to think about it from a woman's perspective, we may see it more clearly.

Men's privilege or entitlement has a long history and is supported by many structures in our society.

Mostly it is about the attitudes that men hold towards women.

Sometimes these attitudes come out in the open, for example when a woman stands for election as a country's leader.

How common is it to hear someone say, "I just don't think it's a job for a woman."

The idea of male privilege is behind this.

"This is a man's job. Men should be the leaders."

For Ron and Liz, it is these beliefs that create the context for Ron's violence towards Liz.

It doesn't cause his violence.

He makes a decision to be violent based on what he believes.

And in our wider society, it is ideas and beliefs like this that form the context for men's violence more broadly.

FOURTEEN

Masculinity and violence

Many men have grown up with an idea that it is wrong to ever hit a girl or a woman.

"I would never hit a woman" is something that I have often heard men say.

Strangely, I have also heard this from men who have actually hit or punched their partners.

Children are often taught not to hit or punch another child.

But there is also so much that children see around them that tells them that violence is ok.

What we teach children, especially boys, about using violence, is often a mixed message.

We don't hear men saying: "I was always told as a child that it is wrong to hit another boy."

If we look at the statistics on men's violence against

other men we find that alarming numbers of men are victims of violence from other men.

The idea of men using their physical strength as a way of standing up for themselves against other men is seen as a normal, understandable and acceptable way for men to behave.

Being able to fight and stand up for yourself is thought to be an important part of being a real man.

Masculinity and violence seem to go hand in hand.

Let's put this into a simple family example.

A young boy, maybe eight or nine years old, comes home from school and his dad asks him how school was today.

He starts to cry.

When Dad asks him what is wrong, he starts to tell him about a group of boys who have been bullying him.

What advice do you think dad is going to give him?

If we did a survey of dads across the country and asked them how they would handle this situation, what do you think they would say?

Many dads are likely to tell their sons something like:

"The only way to stop him, is to go back and show

him who is boss, give it to them, stand up to them, then they will leave you alone."

This response is linked to ideas of what it means to be a man, a "real" man.

If you are going to grow up to be a "real" man, you have to be able to fight and stand up for yourself.

What do we hear when a boy or a man steps away from a fight?

Often it is things like, "Don't be a girl, don't be a pussy, what a wuss."

This is all about the idea of masculinity, the way that we think about being men, being male.

There is a very strong link between masculinity and violence.

This link is another aspect of the context of men's violence against women.

Before we go much further it might be useful to spend a little time thinking about bullying.

It is interesting to think about the link between boys bullying each other and men's violence against women.

Were you ever bullied as a kid?

Did you ever bully other boys?

How does bullying work?

Normally a group of boys will get together to pick on another boy who is different in some way.

He might be a new boy in the class. He might be smaller. He might be from a different cultural background. He might not be good at sport. He might be shy.

The bullies get their power by banding together, being a part of the group.

It often starts with name calling and put downs.

It soon builds to pushing and shoving and then hitting.

Bullying is really an abuse of power against someone who is thought to be less powerful.

There is a strong parallel between bullying and men's violence against women.

The link between masculinity and violence is seen again.

It is as though the idea of being a man has been defined and set in concrete, as though there is a blueprint, an ideal, for how men should be.

This "blueprint" has been set over time.

What does it look like?

This might be an interesting point for you to stop and reflect for a few minutes about the "blueprint" that you grew up with about how men should be.

Did you ever hear something like the idea of "being a real man"?

What did this mean to you?

What did you hear about how "real men" should be?

Write a list of all of the things you were told or picked up along the way.

When you put all of these ideas together, this is your own personal blueprint for masculinity.

I often ask men to think about the ideas that they have grown up with about being a male.

What are the messages boys are given by their parents, teachers and friends, or from movies, TV, magazines, about how boys and men should be?

The answers are predictable: men should be strong, tough, leaders, good at sport, able to drink and hold their drink, good at sex, have ripped bodies, with great muscles, not be afraid to fight. There may be things that you want to add.

This blueprint for masculinity is a big part of the context of men's violence.

This "blueprint" - that we all contribute to in some way - about how males should be, is very powerful.

But how real is this masculinity blueprint?

Sport is a good example where we see this.

One thing I have noticed is that when there is a football match being advertised on TV, we are shown scenes of the last time the teams clashed.

And the focus is on all of the hard tackles and clashes, even on the fights.

Loud music, rapid repeat shots of the toughest tackles, the agro moments, any punches that flew.

All of it is promoted as an exciting game soon to be enjoyed.

And the possibility of a good stand up fight gets the fans even more excited.

The message is: "the tougher the game, the bigger the fights, then the better the whole experience".

Sport is one area of our lives where violence between men is regarded as acceptable, and to some extent at least, a part of being a "real man".

There is a mixed message here. Violence is often actively condemned by sporting organisations. At the same time it is also often promoted as part of the excitement and thrill of the match.

There are many other experiences in boy's, young men's and adult men's lives where violence is normalized.

It is not hard to find other examples of this.

To begin with, you could look at movies and TV shows, video and computer games and boy's toys.

It does not take long to see that there is a strong link between being male, "masculinity", and using violence.

Breaking this link is a big challenge.

If we want to stop men's violence against women, then we need to do some serious thinking about how we might begin to do this.

As we said earlier, sometimes the argument is used that violence is only natural, it is a part of men's biology, a normal urge that we have as men.

This sounds like an excuse to me, but there may be something to it, some primal urge to protect us from danger or attack.

If this is in fact the way it is, I wonder how we then take the next step of justifying a man's right to use violence against his intimate female partner, as a natural primal tendency.

I also wonder, if there is a natural biological link between being male and being violent, then why is it that some men are never violent?

Why is it that not all men are violent?

What is missed in this argument that it is "only natural" for men to use violence, is that it is also a part of being human to make choices about how to act, how to behave despite natural urges that we might have.

There are so many examples in our daily lives of this

ability for human beings to control natural urges and impulses by deciding to act in a particular way.

How then do we begin to break this link?

How do we raise boys and young men to think differently, to act differently?

What are the key messages that we want boys and adolescent males to absorb and build into their lives, to become adults in the world who are safe and who respect the women and children around them?

Do we want young men growing up with the idea that being violent is a natural part of being a man, that "we can't help it".

Do we want to continue to make excuses for hurting others?

And are there other beliefs that men hold that are also a part of the picture when men hurt the women in their lives?

FIFTEEN

Masculinity and sex

Let's explore the notion of masculinity a little more closely.

There are certain fixed ideas about how men are supposed to be.

These become very clear when we talk about men and sex.

The sexual and erotic aspects of men's lives can be expressed in loving and respectful ways and have the potential to support positive and enjoyable relationships.

Sex becomes a problem though when it is acted out abusively.

It is very common when talking to women about their partner's violence, to hear about the way that sex is used abusively against them.

The way that men think about themselves, and how

they should be in the world, is often linked to being sexual.

It is especially linked to the idea of the "phallus".

This refers to the penis, normally as an erect penis, and mostly as a symbol of male potency, power or dominance.

There are many representations of the phallus in our everyday world.

Most modern cities have a tall tower, frequently visited as tourist attractions.

The Eiffel Tower in Paris is a good example.

The taller the tower the better.

Size matters.

Cities compete to have the tallest tower or the tallest building in the world.

Memorial towers, known as obelisks, are also regarded as phallic symbols.

An obelisk in the city of Sydney was recently covered with a large, bright pink condom, in an advertisement for HIV screening tests.

Shiny red sports cars, as well as being thought of as sexy status symbols, are also sometimes regarded as phallic symbols.

Throughout history these common symbols have been designed by men.

Do your own Google search for "phallus" and see what you discover.

It seems that men have been fascinated by the phallus.

If men were truly honest, size matters.

At least to men.

Comparisons are common.

Phrases like "rods of steel" are frequent in men's jokes.

These ideas link sex to power.

The reality for most men though, is that the majority of their lived experience is spent with a soft penis, not a hard, erect penis.

And yet it is the hard, erect penis that seems to define or dictate how men see themselves in the world.

For men undergoing surgery for prostate cancer, one of the big fears is of being "impotent."

The word "potent" is about power and "impotent" means not having power.

In men's health, impotency is the word that is used to describe their inability to have or maintain an erection.

The capacity for a man to have an erection can have a big impact on his self-esteem or identity, and whether he feels ok as a man or not.

The increase in erectile enhancing medications, injections and penile implants, tells us something about how important erections are to the male sense of identity and esteem.

This fear of impotence highlights for us the importance of this particular aspect of the masculinity blueprint.

The links between the phallus and masculinity, and between masculinity and violence are very clear.

Often the way that men use their sexual energy against others is abusive and harmful.

If we go back to the masculinity blueprint, we do not have to look for long to find that a large part of the blueprint sets out how men should be sexually.

There are ideas of sexual power.

- Sexual aggression.
- Being on top.
- Being in charge.
- Being bigger.
- Penetration.
- Domination.
- Force.
- Coercion.
- Rape.

What is sometimes regarded as men expressing themselves naturally, in a sexual way, also has the potential to be abusive.

Primal urges, or natural sexual expressions, can actually be an abuse of power.

When sex, power, entitlement and a lack of consent combine, then the result is abusive.

As social media becomes a part of our everyday lives it is not surprising to find that it is also being used as another way that men, young men and adolescents can abuse women. In a recent survey of over 1,000 women, more than half of them reported being harassed sexually via social media. This was even more serious for women under 30, with 3 out of 4 reporting this experience. They reported being sent explicit sexual photos, being asked to send explicit photos of themselves and being asked to perform sexual acts.

Throughout history men have misused their sexual power as instruments of abuse against women.

This is a sad and shocking history that we as men carry.

The masculinity blueprint supports men having power over women, and in particular, in a sexual way.

How do we repair the hurt, harm and damage that we have done to women, and sadly too often to children, both girls and boys, with our sexual bodies?

Part of the answer to this question is that we begin to challenge and change the ideas that we hold, and which we pass on, about masculinity and sex.

SIXTEEN

A summary: where have we explored so far?

We have covered some pretty big territory.

We have put our focus on men's violence against women.

We have not been side-tracked from talking about this one big issue.

We have worked out why it is not helpful to think about what causes men's violence.

Instead, we have suggested that it is more helpful to think about the context of men's violence.

We have listened to what some men say about their beliefs that underpin their violence.

We have heard them talk about their beliefs about being a man and being superior to women, that they have a right to be in charge, and to have power over women.

We have also talked about the familiar blueprint for

masculinity and the strong link that exists between masculinity and violence.

This is tough territory to cover.

It is tough stuff to think about.

We also have some big ideas to talk about yet, and one of the most important is about how we raise boys to be safe adults, adults who don't hurt the ones they love with violence.

But before we go there, I want to share some other things that I frequently hear from men who have used violence against their intimate female partners.

And sometimes against their children.

There is more to the story.

And if we miss it, we will have missed a really powerful opportunity for change.

SEVENTEEN

Seeing another side to men

When I talk with men who use violence I often hear some surprising contradictions.

On one hand, men will describe their own violent actions.

They will open up and tell me some of the things they have done that have hurt others.

And then, with their next breath, I hear them saying how much their family means to them.

When men say things like this to me I might often not pay much attention.

I might even think they don't mean it, or that they are trying to con me.

It can be easy to miss it, and only hear men's denial of their violence, or how much they blame their partner for their actions, sometimes even playing down what they have actually done.

But there is often much more to the story.

And it is a big story for most men.

This story is the story about being a dad.

"My family mean everything to me."

Lots of men say this.

Lots of men believe this.

Lots of men want to be the best dad they can be.

Men will say things that show how important being a good dad is to them:

- "The reason I work so hard in a job that I hate is for my kids."
- "You know, she is the love of my life."
- "I want us to get ahead, to have a good life."
- "I want more for my kids than what I grew up with."
- "I still remember the day he/she was born."

I wonder what this says about these men.

What does it say about how they see themselves as fathers, how they see themselves as wanting to be good dads?

Men often say that they want to be better dads than what their own fathers were.

"I never wanted to be like my own dad", is a comment I often heard from men.

They talk about their own dad not being there for them, being too busy at work, being hard on them, or not being the sort of man to say, "I love you".

These men clearly want to do it differently.

They want to be different to their own dads.

Some men talk about how strict and harsh their father was with them.

Or even cruel and violent.

I often hear how frightened they were as boys of their own fathers.

The impact of their father's violence still echoes in their life.

When men begin to talk about being dads, they reveal something that is very important to them.

Something deep inside.

In their core.

This idea may be something worth stopping to think about.

Perhaps a good place to start is to think about your own relationship with your dad when you were a kid:

- How did you get on with your dad?

- Were you frightened of him?

- Do you remember him giving you a hug and telling you that he loved you?

- Do you remember when you first started to think about being a dad yourself?

- What ideas did you have about the kind of dad you wanted to be?

- What was that moment like when you first became a father, when you saw your child for the first time?

Being a father is something that most men treasure.

It is very important to us.

There is a unique bond between fathers and their children.

Have you noticed the glow in a man who is about to be a father for the first time.

Often it is quiet.

Understated.

Almost with some shyness.

But it is there nevertheless, as a deep joy and pride.

A joy about being a part of the cycle of life and gifting life to a new individual.

Most fathers really want to be "good dads".

But it is not often talked about openly.

I am imagining a group of men, about half a dozen, talking together about being a dad.

I wonder what this conversation would be like.

I wonder how long it would take to get past the joking and get to the serious, heart-felt experiences.

I wonder what we would really hear men say to each other about being a dad if they were really honest with each other about this.

It is worth thinking about this important part of men's lives.

It is sometimes difficult to hold this reality of wanting to be a good dad alongside the reality that some men hurt their families with their violence.

How does what they say about being a good dad fit with the way that they use violence?

What judgements do we hold about men who use violence in their families?

Do we criticise them?

Do we write them off?

Do we judge them as being unable to change?

Some people believe that men who use violence

against their intimate female partners are basically bad people.

They hurt their partners.

They hurt their kids.

They must be bad.

To believe that men who hurt others are bad, is too simple a view.

We might not like the things they have done, but the belief that they are bad, is unfair.

And it is not true.

And this belief that we might hold about them creates a huge barrier to being able to see anything that might help them to change.

We might miss seeing the potential for them to change and end their violence towards their families.

Thinking that men who use violence are "monsters" is a huge barrier to creating safety for women and children.

If you are reading this, and you are a man who has hurt your partner or your kids, I wonder what you believe about yourself.

What you think about yourself is more important than what anybody else thinks about you.

I wonder if you think you are bad, or a "monster".

I wonder what you think about whether you are a good dad or not.

I wonder how you fit your hopes of being a good dad with the reality that you have hurt your kids and their mother.

(It is important to remember that kids are hurt when their mother is hurt.)

I wonder how you fit these two realities together in your own mind.

You might think, "I really do want to be a good dad, my family means everything to me, but I know that I hurt them with my violence."

I think it would be good for us to talk about this for a while.

I am interested to hear the way that you think about yourself, your fathering and your violence.

EIGHTEEN

What goes on inside

I want to talk about feelings.

Emotions.

This may be something that is not easy for you, but let's give it a go.

I would like us to talk about your own internal reactions when you use violence.

How do you react?

What do you think, what do you say to yourself inside your head?

What do you notice inside yourself?

I am interested in all of the mixed emotions you might have tumbling around inside.

The idea of talking about internal reactions probably sounds a bit strange.

It might feel like an odd thing to do.

But there is most likely a mix of things going on inside.

Let's do it this way.

Maybe think about a time when you know that you have said or done something that has really hurt your partner, either physically or emotionally. That is, you have hit her either with your hands or with your words.

One of the first reactions you might have is to blame your partner.

You might be saying things inside your head like, "She ought to know better by now that I don't like being interrupted."

Or it might be something like, "I get really tired by the end of a long week, and I need my down time. There is only so much I can take. If only she would learn to give me some space, I wouldn't get so wound up."

Your first thoughts might be something like this.

You might be in the habit of blaming your partner.

But I want us to get past making excuses and blaming to go a bit deeper, perhaps to thoughts and feelings that you may have not really talked about before. Maybe you are like other men who say, "I never wanted to be like my own dad!"

This may give us a clue to something going on inside.

It may be that you are feeling disappointed in yourself, as though you have let yourself down.

Disappointed in yourself.

That is one possible reaction.

It is possible that there are other reactions too.

Let's go back to the idea that I hear from some men, "It is wrong to hit a girl or a woman."

We could ask ourselves about the reaction that men might have when they have in fact done this and broken their own code.

It is possible that men might feel very embarrassed by their own actions.

They would not want anyone else to know what they have done.

They would not tell anyone.

They would not tell their mates.

Disappointed. Embarrassed. What else might be possible?

Thinking again about the things that I have heard men say about their own violence, I often hear men use the simple words, "I felt so bad!"

This is often followed by an immediate apology.

So what do we make of his feelings - disappointed, embarrassed, bad?

Are they real or not?

Are they genuine?

I wonder if the word "regret" fits in here.

Sometimes feelings of regret might not seem real, especially if they are followed by more violence later on.

Regret is linked to feeling guilty.

So putting all of this together, it is very likely that there is a lot going on inside a man following his violent actions that may not be obvious.

On the surface, what is obvious is blaming and making excuses.

But underneath there is probably a lot going on.

What would happen if we took these reactions seriously, instead of ignoring them or dismissing them?

We might find an even stronger emotion underneath that might need to be talked about.

And it might tell us something very important about this man.

NINETEEN

The hidden emotion

If you had the word "shame" in your mind you were right.

Underneath all of the emotions we have just talked about, shame is often sitting deep inside.

Shame.

What an interesting word.

It is thought to have its early meaning in an old word that meant "to cover".

When we think about it, a natural, almost immediate response for any of us, when we do something that we are not happy with is "to cover" it.

Shame is the strongest feeling that I have heard from men when they are talking about their violence.

And this often becomes the turning point for them.

When men are able to talk about how important being a dad is to them, and then link this to the shame that they carry deep inside for their use of violence, they face the possibility of change.

It is when our own actions clash with our own values that shame creeps in.

Shame is basically the feeling we have inside when we have done something that we think is bad, and that we are unhappy about.

We want to cover it up.

We do not want other people to know about it.

If we go back to your own reactions following a time when you have been controlling, abusive, or perhaps physically violent to your partner, you may have felt bad, disappointed, guilty, and perhaps, underlying all of this, ashamed.

If you are acknowledging this to yourself now, then this is helpful.

There is no shame in expressing shame.

It is probably one of the most important things you could do.

So what does a man do with his own feelings of shame when he has hurt his partner?

As you are reading this, I am wondering about your own thoughts about this idea of shame.

I am wondering if you have thought about this before.

I am wondering whether shame is the really deep down feeling that you have when you hurt your partner.

I am also wondering what you do with this feeling of shame.

For any person, feelings of shame are tough to deal with.

Shame does not want to see the light of day.

Nor does it want the glare of judgement from others.

Shame wants to stay hidden.

In the dark.

Out of sight.

So what does it mean to put shame out in the open?

Putting shame out in the open means facing it head on.

Admitting it to yourself first.

And then taking the courageous step of admitting it to someone else.

It is best if it is someone who will not further shame you for your shame.

One of the reasons for wanting to hide our shame is because we are afraid of being further shamed.

This is especially true if we have hurt others.

And we often think that there is nothing we can do about the fact that we have hurt someone else.

And it is true, we cannot change the reality of our past actions that have hurt others.

But for men who have been violent to their partners and children, facing their shame can often be the beginning of change.

This probably sounds like quite a strange thing to say.

You may be wondering how facing shame could possibly be a turning point.

This is because to face shame, someone has to own up to what they have done.

Speaking up honestly about having hurt someone is a part of taking the lid off the shame.

Some people think that it isn't necessary to go over old ground.

They put their heads in the sand.

They think it will go away.

But shame is not like that.

It doesn't just go away.

If shame is kept hidden it bubbles away inside and finds its way out.

But it finds its way out with negative feelings.

Maybe anger.

Or depression.

Or more cover up.

It's probably a bit different for everyone.

It might be worth thinking about your own feelings of shame and what you do with them.

And how they might find their way out in unhelpful ways.

Or worth thinking about what it means for you that you keep that shame deep inside, hidden, out of sight.

If you begin to pay attention to the possibility that you may feel shame deep inside, you will begin to understand more.

If you admit it to yourself, and begin to notice it, you will see it more clearly.

You will see how it affects you and how it finds its own way out in unhelpful ways.

I wonder what you are thinking right now about your own feelings of shame.

I wonder what you are thinking about what you

normally do with these feelings.

I am wondering if you think there is something else that you can do with these feelings.

I am wondering if you have ever begun to face these feelings head on.

It may be useful to do some thinking about what you can do about any feelings of shame that you might have.

Can you imagine getting together with your best mate to have a serious talk with him about your violence?

Can you imagine looking him fair and square in the eye as you tell him about the last time you hit your partner or abused her and called her names?

What would it be like for you to do this?

Thinking about the possibility of doing this might give you a bit of an idea about how much shame you carry.

There are probably lots of suggestions I could give you about what to do with your shame, but your own ideas will be the best ideas.

How about making a couple of dot points about what you think.

Or even write down the names of one or two mates who you might want to talk to.

It also may be useful to think about how doing

something about your feelings of shame may lead you forward to a place where you stop hurting your partner.

It might be the turning point that you are looking for.

This is the goal.

Stopping your violence and abuse.

Making life safe for your family.

TWENTY

Breaking the Cycle

What can we learn from other men about how to end their violence against their female partners?

There must be some men who have faced their shame, broken the cycle, stopped their violence and changed their behaviours.

What could these men tell us that will help other men to end their violence?

I wonder what they would say was the trigger for them to change.

What would have given them the realisation that helped them to stop hurting their partner?

How did they get help?

And where from?

For most of these men, something has happened that is a trigger for change.

It may have been a partner leaving, the police getting involved and taking police action, sending someone to Emergency or family or neighbours getting involved.

It may have been some other kind of wake-up call that they have had.

Sometimes it takes a crisis to get us to take action.

Sadly, too often, some crises only make things worse.

Instead of being a turning point for change, some men increase their violence.

As men, we are generally not good at putting our hands up and asking for help.

We have a pretty bad record when it comes to our own health care.

We tend to put things off and think it will all be ok.

I wonder if this is a part of the blueprint that we talked about earlier.

The idea that we ought to be able to take care of ourselves, tough it out, sort things out and fix problems without help.

Reading this book may be the first time that you have decided that you want to make a change.

Hopefully, it will be one of many decisions that you will make towards living without violence.

I think this is the key.

Making a decision to live without violence.

We live in a society that is filled with violence and, as we have already noticed, there seems to be a strong link between being a man and being violent.

When it is all boiled down, it is possible to nip violence in the bud, to stop it before it really gets started.

I noticed it myself recently.

I took my Mum out shopping.

Pushing her through the shopping centre in her wheelchair, people got in my way.

I noticed my aggravation, frustration, judgement and muttering under my breath at people walking along with no awareness of us at all.

It was my right to have free movement in the shopping centre and they were in my way.

They should move.

They should not stop right in front of me and block my path.

Can't they see us?

Why can't they keep to the left?

Go to another scene, where this is obvious.

Driving on the roads.

Someone cuts in front of me, changes lanes without using his blinker.

How do I react?

I don't have to tell you.

What am I muttering at the other driver?

"What right does he have? This is my lane."

But is it?

Do I own the road?

Or is the road there to be shared between drivers and cyclists and pedestrians?

We could multiply this scene many times.

But you have got the point.

Violence is fundamentally a **state of mind** a belief in my own rights, my own importance or power or position.

And if this gets trodden on by anybody, I think I have a right to push back, speak out or lash out.

And I behave accordingly, unless I decide to act differently, and let go of my belief that I have a right to own the road, or the footpath or whatever it is that I want to control.

Come back to the shopping centre scene with my mum.

As soon as I noticed my pattern of thoughts and muttering under my breath, I took some action to change it.

I noticed it.

I thought about it.

I made a decision.

I let go of my thoughts about my rights being more important than the rights of other shoppers.

I began to pay attention to the other shoppers and I changed the look on my face to more of a smile than a frown.

This is where we start.

Noticing the pattern.

Being fully aware, noticing and then admitting the truth to ourselves.

It takes courage to admit the truth to ourselves.

It takes guts to be honest with ourselves.

I am presuming that you have had the courage to keep reading to this point.

This tells me that you have the guts, the strength to decide not to use violence.

It tells me that you really want something different for your partner and your children.

It tells me that you want to stop using violent, abusive and controlling actions that hurt others.

To decide that you want to stop hurting the ones you love is the most important decision you can make.

This is the beginning of your new path.

Kind man.

Strong man.

The two go together.

Being strong enough to face up to your actions.

Being strong enough to face your shame.

Being strong enough to let go of the need to be in charge.

Being strong enough to not use violence, or to use abuse as a way of staying on top.

Being strong enough to be kind to others.

Kind man.

Strong man.

TWENTY-ONE

On track

As you begin to walk this new path you may need some help.

Professional help.

Help from someone who understands the issues clearly and will challenge and encourage you to stay on the path.

Finding help may be tough depending on where you live.

You will need to find someone you can meet with regularly who can listen to you and hear you without shaming you.

Finding someone who you can begin to talk honestly with about your own violence and controlling behaviours is going to help you as you walk this path.

You might think it is better just to move forward

rather than going back over the old ground of your past actions.

This "old ground of past actions" is important though because it holds the key to your patterns - what you think, what you want, what beliefs you hold.

Knowing your own patterns helps you to notice what is going on inside.

And noticing what is going on inside is helpful in making better choices in the future.

It is also important because it is a way of facing up to your past actions.

Some people call this "taking responsibility".

Facing up honestly to your past actions has a two-way impact.

It helps to put you on a positive path for the future.

More importantly, it supports your partner's healing from the hurt that you have caused.

This is not the end of the path though.

It is a beginning.

The big question is how to continue to walk this path of courage.

No empty apologies.

No blanket apologies, "I am sorry for any time I have hurt you."

No apologies that blame the person for being hurt, "I am sorry if that hurt you."

No half-baked promises to be different.

They don't work and you have tried them all before.

This may be a good time to ask you to work out your own ideas for this path.

What would it look like, what steps would you take if you wanted to stop using violence and put things right in your family so that they all feel safe and no longer afraid of you?

This is an important question to think about.

Nobody knows better than you about yourself and how you operate.

So before I give you my thoughts about this, it would be helpful for you to spend some time working on this.

This is a path of courage.

It is a path well worth walking, because it is a path that will bring safety to your family.

It is a path that will see you become a kind man, a strong man.

TWENTY-TWO

A path of courage

As we begin to think about making a change, I am interested to know what ideas you have.

What ideas have you come up with about what you can do to end your violence?

As we have said, it takes courage to face up to our past actions, to change and to put things right.

It would be so much easier to walk away, start again, blame your partner, blame everything else in your life, get together with your mates, hit the grog, have a big whinge about women, feminism, political correctness, police, courts, kids, bosses, society, everything.

And nothing will change.

But stopping and having a look inside at what is really going on, and looking honestly at what you have done, and how your actions have hurt your family, that takes courage.

It takes guts.

Courage is a great word.

It comes from the same word as the French word for heart, "coeur". To do something to end your violence and build a safe home for your family is heart work.

This may sound like a really strange thing to say: "heart work".

What I mean is that the hard work that is needed comes from deep down inside you.

It is motivated by the things that you want most in your life, the things that are most important to you. It comes from the very core of your being, from your heart, what you most long for and value.

It is about being the kind of dad that you really want to be, the kind of partner that you really want to be.

There are three main steps involved.

They are linked together, they flow from one to the other.

Put simply they are:

- Face up to what you have done
- Know how you have hurt others
- Repair the damage you have done.

This is the path.

The next three chapters will look in more detail at each one of these steps.

But that is it in a nutshell.

The point is that these three steps will need to become a part of what you think about and act on each day.

I have heard some men say, "I have said sorry. Why isn't that enough?

Why can't she just get over it and move on?"

It would be great if it were so simple.

But it is not.

Many women who have been affected by their partner's violence say, "I just want him to take responsibility for his violence."

They want his violence to stop, but they mean a lot more.

They also mean that they want him to own up to the things he has done to hurt and abuse and control them.

They want him to really understand how his violence has affected them, what its full impact has been.

And they also want him to start taking some positive steps to putting things right, to fixing up what has been broken or damaged.

This is the full meaning of taking responsibility for your violence.

TWENTY-THREE

Facing up

Facing up is the first important step in doing something to end your violence for good.

You cannot skip this step.

It is not meant to make you feel bad about what you have done.

The purpose is so that you know fully and clearly what actions you are stopping, and what you are facing up to.

And also that your partner knows that you know.

One way to think about this is to imagine that someone has broken into your house and stolen many of your possessions.

You have called the police and they have come to investigate.

They end up catching the thief.

But none of what has been stolen is returned.

And the really valuable, precious items are still missing.

They have not been returned and the person who stole them denies that they were ever stolen.

What you need is for the thief to come clean.

Many men will make a blanket apology, "I am sorry if I have hurt you."

But being specific about what you are apologising for is much more powerful.

And it makes a big difference.

What is needed in this step is a full and frank uncovering of all of your actions that have hurt your partner or have controlled her or abused her in some way.

One way to do this might be to do a timeline of your relationship.

Buy a note book and use a double page for every year of your relationship.

Start to write down all the things that you can remember that you have done that have hurt her.

You might have some trouble remembering.

But these are your notes.

Don't ask your partner to tell you or remember them for you.

This is your job, not hers.

Remember, when we are talking about your violence we are talking about much more than your physical violence.

We are talking about all of the ways that you have used to hurt her, control her or abuse her.

Let's break it down into categories, starting with physical abuse.

You could include hitting or pushing or knocking her out of the way.

Throwing things or slamming doors.

Bashing your fists on the table.

Knocking over a chair.

Punching walls.

Kicking her, kicking things or hurting pets.

Driving fast or dangerously.

Sometimes these actions include verbal abuse too.

Shouting.

Swearing.

Calling her names.

Giving orders.

Verbal abuse often goes hand in hand with mental abuse.

Blaming her for what you have done.

Making her think she is crazy.

Constant criticism and finding fault in everything she does.

Attacking her self-esteem, telling her she is hopeless and pathetic.

Making mean remarks about her body.

Making all the big decisions.

Controlling what she eats or what she wears.

Whether she can have chocolate in the house.

And something that no-one talks about much is sexual abuse in the relationship.

Pestering her for sex.

Forcing her to have sex when she says no.

Rape.

Forcing her to do sexual things that she doesn't want to do.

Humiliating her sexually in front of friends by criticising her.

The list is not complete without some of the more subtle forms of control.

Women often describe the way that they have been gradually and deliberately isolated from their family and friends.

This includes moving away from being close to other family members.

Being critical of them.

Not allowing family to visit, or allowing her to visit them.

Insulting family and friends and having fights with them so they stay away.

Stopping her from driving or having access to a car.

All of these actions come under the heading of "social abuse".

Financial abuse is another control tactic.

It takes many forms.

Not giving her any money and keeping control of all of the finances, or making her responsible for handling all of the bills and being critical of her for not doing it properly.

Criticising her for buying things for herself or for the kids.

Spiritual abuse is also common.

This might be by putting her down for her religious beliefs or practices.

Stopping her from attending meetings or services.

Or it might be even by forcing her to observe religious practices against her will.

So if you have a notebook and have started thinking about all of the ways you may have hurt your partner, you have made a start.

A good start.

By completing this timeline you are increasing your own awareness of all of the different ways that you have hurt or controlled your partner, and how you have done this over time.

It will be interesting to notice if there are any patterns in the things you have done.

How and when did it start?

Has it got worse over time?

More frequent?

More intense or serious?

Have you started to use different forms of abuse?

It might also be useful to work out how you have denied your violence and abuse.

Sometimes it is easy to argue away some of your actions:

"That's not really abusive. That's not what I meant. I was only joking."

You may also have tried to blame your partner for your actions,

"If only she would realise when I am stressed out and just back off."

"If she could just get off my back and leave me alone."

"She should know when to steer clear of me."

Another thing that you might do is to play down your violence,

"I only hit her once."

"It wasn't that hard."

"It was just a tap."

Blaming your partner is another way of controlling her.

It is abusive.

It hurts your partner.

So does ignoring or denying what you have done or playing it down.

Saying things that make it her fault when it isn't, does damage.

Saying that you have not done anything, does damage.

Saying it's not that bad, does damage.

So back to the list you are working on.

Don't do anything with your list at the moment.

Keep thinking about it.

Keep being honest with yourself.

Keep adding to the list as more things come to your mind.

When you are ready to start thinking about the next step you will be able to use these notes that you have worked on so far.

The next step is to work out how your actions have hurt others.

TWENTY-FOUR

What harm have I caused?

There are three groups of people who have been affected by your violence:

Your partner.

Your children.

Yourself.

You might like to go back to the notebook that you used in the last chapter where you began to write about all of your past actions that have hurt others.

I suggested that you do this like a timeline.

This gives a good idea of any patterns that have developed, especially if you have been in a number of relationships.

If you go back over the notes that you have written, you could use a different coloured pen to add in some comments about the impact your violence is having on those close to you.

This is a good next step.

It is really worth trying to think about this for yourself.

As we said earlier, it would be easier to ask your partner about how it affected her.

But that means she would be doing the work for you.

It would probably make a real difference for her if you did this work and thought about it for yourself.

To do this you might have to see things through your partner's eyes.

You might have to walk in her shoes, know what it is like from her side.

How will you begin to do this?

You may have spent a long time seeing your partner as the problem, the one who needs to change and do things differently.

Be a better mother.

Do better in the house.

Be more interested in sex.

Take more care about how she looks, what she wears, what she eats.

You may have been very critical of her with put-downs.

How do you get to know what it has been like for her living with your violence?

How do you get to know what it has been like for your kids living with your violence?

And have you ever stopped to think about the impact of your violence on yourself?

You may have been telling yourself that things aren't that bad, that they will get over it, that you are not as bad as some blokes that you know.

They should all see how lucky they are.

It's a tough thing to do to see clearly how you have really hurt them, on the inside as well as on the outside.

I remember clearly one woman telling me how much her partner hated her having friends.

He didn't like them.

She had one good friend who lived across the street from her.

When she would go to see her she would always sit at the front window to watch if he came home early.

She knew he always parked his ute around the back of the house.

This would give her time to get back home before he got inside.

She was frightened of him.

He was a good bloke with a good business.

She liked him a lot.

But she knew she would pay for it if she broke any of his rules.

Sometimes this would be with slaps across the face or a lot of criticism about her being lazy and doing nothing to help him and sitting around all day with her friends.

She never knew when he would start on at her about something that broke his rules.

She didn't tell people about how frightened she was of him, because he was everybody's best mate.

He always put on a good front.

Everyone thought he was a great bloke.

But she lived in fear.

She also started to lose friends because she would never ask them to her place.

She would never even think about going out with her friends on a girls' night.

She began to lose confidence in herself.

She hated how she looked because of his constant

comments about her body.

She thought she was ugly and fat.

There is an important step to take here, and that is to be clear about how your actions have actually affected your partner and your kids.

How are you going with this so far?

I have encouraged you to try and think about this for yourself and try to work it out, to see things from her side, to put yourself in her shoes.

One way to do this is to watch and listen.

What do you notice about your partner's reactions to you?

Has the way that she likes to be with you changed over time?

Does she pull away from you when you want to be close?

Does she seem afraid of you at times?

Does she feel safe when she is with you?

I am wondering if you are enjoying your relationship in the same way you did when you first got together.

And what about your kids?

We could ask the same questions?

Have you noticed times when they seem really scared of you and what you might do to them?

Do you notice them pull away from you sometimes?

Do you think that your kids feel safe around you?

Have they stopped giving you hugs or wanting hugs from you?

There is a lot that I could write here to tell you about how men's violence affects every member of their families.

There is a lot of research on this subject.

If you want to read some of this you can do a Google search.

You might like to look at a helpful website aimed at preventing violence against women and children: www.ourwatch.org.au

But I think you already know about the impact on your partner.

You have been living with these impacts.

Have you been noticing?

Have you been seeing?

Have you been listening?

Have you been hearing?

The more that you notice, the more you will see.

As you let go of blaming her for everything and making excuses for yourself, you will begin to see more clearly what your words and actions have done.

You have also been living with the impact of your own violence on yourself.

Maybe this is something that you have never stopped to think about.

But it is worth taking some time to do it.

It is likely that no-one else has really talked with you honestly about this either.

I am pretty sure that you are not happy with yourself, that you don't like what you do and how you hurt the people you love.

I know that this is something that you can change.

I also know that it is possible to find ways to repair the harm or damage that you have done to others.

TWENTY-FIVE

Repairing the harm

How does someone rebuild trust in someone who has let them down?

How does someone get to feel safe again with someone who has frightened them so much?

How does someone get to believe in herself again after being told for so long that she is hopeless or no good?

How do kids learn to love someone again after they have been hurt so much that they start to hate?

How do kids start to feel proud of their dad again after he has hurt them and their mum?

These are really tough questions.

But they are just the beginning.

A lot of the damage or harm that you may have

caused is physical – bruising, black eyes, broken bones.

Physical harm often heals.

It is the emotional harm that is deeper, maybe unseen, but very, very real, where the hard work of repair needs to be done.

You can probably see by now that the three steps that I have been describing are all wrapped up together.

It is not a matter of doing step one, moving on to step two and then to number three, one after the other.

Repairing the harm means that you keep going with all three, all at the same time.

They are in a bundle together and each one affects the other.

Saying "sorry" is never enough by itself to repair the harm that you have done.

It is no good just facing up to something you have done if you don't do something to repair the damage.

As I keep on saying, this is **your** work to do.

It is important that you work out for yourself how you will repair the damage that you have caused.

I could give you some ideas.

Your partner or kids could give you some ideas.

But other people's ideas will not work.

They need to be your ideas.

They need to come from you.

Every man reading this book faces a different situation.

The ways that you have hurt others are different.

You are different to other men.

Your partner and your kids are all different.

You know them all best.

And you know how you have hurt them.

So your ideas on how to repair the harm are the ones that will work best.

Maybe you can go back to the notebook you have been writing in.

The timeline that you have done might give you some clues about where to start the repair work.

I have suggested using a different coloured pen for noting down how you have hurt your partner and your kids.

You could use another colour as you try to figure out how to repair the harm you have caused.

Before we go any further, it may seem like a really obvious thing to say, but it will be impossible to repair anything if your violence continues.

You will not be able to repair the harm you have caused, if you keep on hurting them with further violence or abuse.

You will need to really put yourself under the microscope and see all of the ways that you abuse or control your partner and your kids.

And how this has hurt them.

And you will need to stop.

You will need to stop hitting, hurting, abusing, controlling.

You cannot do the repair work if you keep on hurting them.

Let me say it this way, every time you raise your voice, or call your partner a name, or use any of your old behaviours, will put them back to square one.

Their trust and safety will be broken.

This doesn't mean that you cannot make mistakes.

But it is being genuine about change and working hard to make that change that will help you and them recover.

There is nothing that we can do to change what we have done in the past, but it is possible to take some steps towards repairing the harm that has been caused.

You are the only person responsible for this repair work.

You and your actions have done the damage.

It is yours to repair.

But there are some traps along the way.

The best way to think about these traps is to think about the words - minimise, deny and blame - that we talked about earlier.

You will probably be tempted to say something like, "But if only she would (add your own ending)."

You can avoid these traps by noticing the things you think inside your head, or the words you actually say.

When you start to say, "But …" then you probably have an excuse about to start. It is probably followed by something about what your partner does or does not do.

There are some other words to listen for as well.

One common way of making an excuse starts with thoughts like:

"I was just…"

"It wasn't really…" or

"I was only…" or

"She is such a…"

There are quite a few of these different ways that you might use to shift responsibility onto your partner for your actions.

Doing this is, in fact, another way that you might abuse or control your partner.

Whenever you minimise or deny your violence, or blame it on someone else, you are using another form of power that is abusive and controlling.

You are adding further hurt rather than doing the repair work.

If you think about it from your partner's view, even if you have stopped hitting or hurting her but you tell her it was all her fault, this will inflict more hurt and it will make it harder for her to trust you again.

You are probably realising that the repair work has a lot of twists and turns.

It is not straightforward.

It would be helpful to turn our thoughts to the heart of the repair work.

TWENTY-SIX

Safety, Safety, Safety

At the very heart of the repair work is safety.

If the thing that we want most, at the very core of our beings, at the very heart of things, is to be the safest dads we can be, the safest husbands or partners, then we are on the right track.

To hold to this commitment will help us to do the repair work as we move forward.

Let's go back to the comments I made earlier about being safe drivers.

It might help to use this as an example of how to rebuild trust, care and safety for our families even after we have hurt them with our violence.

If any of you have been involved in a car accident, you will understand the normal emotions and reactions, when you get back into a car again.

People are often anxious, nervous, on edge, really alert.

As a driver, you are probably thinking carefully about being really safe: sticking to the speed limit, stopping at orange lights, changing lanes carefully, making sure everyone has their seat belts on.

Your attention to driving as safely as possible will help your passengers to trust that they will be safe again.

It might take a while for their experience of the accident to fade, but if they see evidence that you are driving safely, they will begin to feel confident again.

As soon as you start to speed or get uptight and drive dangerously, their fear of another accident will come back.

Fear stays in our bodies.

Fear stays in our thoughts.

Fear sits in our gut.

It takes a long time for the fear of being hurt again to go away.

As soon as they hear you get angry, or starting to swear, or getting edgy or bossy, they will start to feel afraid.

Their bodies are reacting normally to fear.

Living as a safe man in your family is something that you want.

That is why you are still reading.

Making this your clear goal will help you to do the things that are needed for your family to be safe and to not feel frightened of you.

One really helpful way of thinking about safety is the idea of carrying safety **in me** as a man.

I love that thought: carrying safety **IN** me as a dad, as a partner, as a grandad, as a man.

This is not my idea. It is the idea of a colleague of mine.*

She talks about the safety **OF** children, safety **FOR** mothers, and safety **IN** dads. (Thanks M-J*)

This breaks it down into really simple goals:

- I want to ensure the safety **OF** my kids
- I want to build safety **FOR** their mum
- I want to be committed to safety **IN** me.

If you are really serious about being a safe dad, it will help you to notice the things you are doing and saying.

You will notice how they affect the people around you.

Being really serious about being a safe dad, means thinking about it every day.

Making sure it is on your mind, front and centre.

Having something that reminds you every day that this is how you really want to be will help you to stay focussed.

Perhaps when you wake up each morning, when you get out of bed and put your feet on the floor for the first time each day, say to yourself, "Today, I will be a safe dad."

Why not try this, give it a go, just once?

Tomorrow morning, first thing, put your feet on the floor, feel the solid floor under your feet, and say, "Today I will be a safe dad!"

See how it feels.

See what difference it makes.

And give it another try, the day after, and the day after that.

Keep on going.

TWENTY-SEVEN

Watching our words

Words can really hurt.

They can break trust.

We know that what we say and how we say it can, in fact, hurt others.

If we want to re-build safety and trust in our families, then what we say and how we say it becomes important.

Once you have stopped your violence and started the repair work, then what you say and how you say it will be even more important than before.

You will probably begin to notice more than ever before that what you say has an impact on others.

Those around you may still feel frightened by the tone of your voice, by the words you use, by what you say.

Watching out for reactions in your partner and your kids that show they are feeling frightened of you, is a way to keep their safety in mind.

This will be a signal to stop and to be aware of what you are saying and change it, so that they feel safe again.

Back on track.

Being mindful of the way you speak and the words you use will help to repair the harm that you have caused.

Saying sorry, apologising, is another area where our words are important.

It comes very naturally for some people to apologise, to say sorry for something they have done.

For others, it is much more difficult.

Making an apology can sometimes be a bit tricky.

Some men say things like, "I have told her I am sorry. What more does she want?"

I am wondering if you have said this, or perhaps thought this.

I am wondering what you think of these words now.

I am wondering what you would now say differently.

Women often tell me things like, "I am tired of

hearing his apologies. I don't want to hear him say sorry. I don't want to hear his empty promises to never do it again."

This is worth taking notice of because it tells us very clearly how words have to be matched by real and lasting actions.

It is very common for women to describe how their partner reacts to their violence with an apology almost immediately following.

It is a pattern of feeling bad and sorry that comes with an apology and a promise to never do it again.

This becomes meaningless after a while.

They want his violence to stop.

They don't want a broken promise or a half-baked apology.

When we hear people apologising on TV for something they have done, it is easy to pick if they mean it or not.

The difference between an apology that is real and genuine and one that is not, is really obvious:

"If I hurt you, I am sorry."
"Surely you realise I was only joking."
"I didn't mean it. You should know that."

These apologies do not sound genuine.

They don't help to repair.

You know the difference.

You have heard people apologising and you know they haven't meant it.

It is really easy to pick.

There is often an "if/but" of some kind.

The "if/but" is a give-away:

- "If you are hurt."
- "But you are always so sensitive."
- "But you have taken it the wrong way."
- "If you didn't understand."

Changing the way that you speak about your violence and the way that you apologise, will be a part of the repair work.

Thinking about making a meaningful apology, that is backed up by changed actions, will help.

So, what are the ingredients of a meaningful apology?

- Words and actions will match
- Others will not be blamed
- You will admit what you have done

- You will show that you understand the way your actions have been hurtful

- There will be no empty promises

- You will take responsibility for what you have said or done

- You will not expect or demand forgiveness

- You will take action to change.

Here is an example of what a genuine apology might sound like:

"Yesterday when I swore at you and called you that name, "*#|¥<#>". I was wrong.

I know that you got worried that I was getting worked up.

I could see that you were scared that I would do something worse.

I could see that the kids were scared too.

I am sorry."

You might also want to add something like:

"I want this to change.

I do not want to do and say things that hurt and frighten you.

I am very sorry.

I have let you down and I have let myself down.

I am not asking you to forgive me or to be patient with me.

I realise that I wanted you to do something that you didn't want to do.

I was trying to control you. I realise that now.

I am beginning to understand how often I do that and how it affects you.

I want to stop hurting you and controlling you."

Wow, that is long-winded isn't it?

Much harder than "sorry, it won't happen again".

Yes, but it has all the ingredients:

- What I did
- How it hurt you
- I want to repair the hurt.

No hollow words or empty promises.

No grand commitments.

No expectations of forgiveness or trust.

But an understanding of how your actions have hurt others.

Working on getting an apology to be meaningful and genuine is a part of the repair work.

There have probably been many times when you have said sorry for your actions and then some time later done the same thing again.

This breaks trust.

TWENTY-EIGHT

Re-building trust

By now you are getting a clear idea that the repair work will take time.

It is slow and gradual.

The most important part of this work is getting back to a place where your partner and your kids trust you again.

I am guessing that what you really want is for them to know without question that they are safe with you:

- That you will not hurt them.

- That they do not need to be frightened of you.

- That they can joke around and have fun with you, without you suddenly getting cranky.

- That they can play with you without being hurt. Or called horrible names.

- Or be put down for not doing something the right way.

What you really want is for them to be able to trust that you will be kind to them.

Trust is such a big word.

It goes hand in hand with safety.

Safety and trust.

Trust can be so easily broken and it is so hard to rebuild once it has been broken.

It is important as you re-build trust that you stay on track.

Maybe a helpful way to think about this is like going on a mountain trek.

Sometimes this can be tricky.

There might be rough, steep sections.

There might be unsafe bridges crossing raging streams.

There might be many hazards or side-tracks.

You might want to give up and go back.

Or just stop.

Staying on track and not giving up is crucial.

It means being the person you really want to be in your family.

Determining how you want to be as a dad, every day.

Ask yourself:

"What kind of connection do I want to have with my kids and with my partner?"

"Do I want my family to feel safe with me?"

"Do I want my family to **be safe** with me?"

"Do I want them to know without a doubt that I will be kind to them?"

I am reminded again about the many men who tell me that they want to be better fathers than their own dads.

They want to be different.

This not only tells us that their dad's actions perhaps had a negative impact on them.

It also tells us that they want to make sure that they do not make the same mistakes.

Making this decision to do it differently means that you have already started to work towards being a kind man, a strong man.

Maybe you have started to make some other decisions.

Maybe you have admitted some things to yourself.

Maybe you have stopped blaming other people for your actions.

Maybe you have looked closely at your past actions and realised that you do not like what you see.

Maybe you have started to really see that your kids and your partner are getting closer to you.

Maybe you are beginning to see some signs that they are not as frightened of you as they once were.

These are all good beginnings.

But they are just that – good beginnings.

It is not the end of the road.

Perhaps you have begun to understand why I have used the words kind man, strong man.

Simply speaking, stopping our violence is about being **kind** to the ones we love, our partner, and our kids.

Kindness and violence cannot exist together.

Strong man.

It takes real strength to face up to the hurt that you have caused.

It takes real strength to face the truth about what you have done and to set about repairing the damage.

It takes real strength to keep at it and to build safety and trust back into your family.

Kind man, strong man.

Do these words describe the man that you want to be in your family?

Kind man: acting kindly, ending your violence, working hard to build safety and trust.

Strong man: having the guts to face up and be honest about how your words and deeds have hurt and having the strength to stick at the hard work of repair.

TWENTY-NINE

Finding support

There may be times when you will start to think about throwing in the towel.

Giving up.

It might all seem too hard.

Staying on track and keeping your focus might seem all too much and you may need someone to support you.

You may need the help of a professional, like a counsellor.

If you decide that you need this kind of support it will be important to find someone who will not let you off the hook and who will not join you in blaming your partner or excusing your actions.

You want a counsellor who will help you to explore your own desire to be the best dad that you can be.

This counsellor will respect you and support you as you change.

Above all else, your counsellor will keep listening for any indications that your partner and children are not safe.

And will keep challenging you to make the changes that you want to make to ensure safety for everyone.

Finding the right counsellor for you can be tricky.

It is ok to keep looking until you find the right one.

The most important quality is that they must have a good understanding of the dynamics of men's violence and, as I just said, they will put a priority on the safety of your partner and children.

And they must know how to respectfully support you as you take the steps to be responsible and accountable as you stop your violence and end your controlling behaviours.

Another thing, and this may be tough to hear, a good counsellor will know the law.

A good counsellor will help you to understand the criminal nature of your violence.

A good counsellor will know about Apprehended Violence Orders (AVOs) or protection orders that may be put in place by the police or the courts to protect your partner and children.

A good counsellor will help you to see the benefit of these orders for your partner and also in supporting you to be a safe dad.

The law exists to support the safety and well-being of everyone, even you.

I have often wondered when a man knows that his violence comes under the criminal code, what stops him from going to the police and seeking help.

I wonder what stops him from going to the police and asking for a protection order to be put in place against himself.

I can hear you laughing at this suggestion.

Who is going to dob himself in for speeding, for example.

But this is a bit different.

If a man really wants to take responsibility for his violence towards his partner, a protection order might be just the thing he needs to give him that extra bit of support or motivation.

It might also be helpful to join a group of men making similar decisions to end their violence.

It will take courage to talk with other men who are walking the same path, asking themselves the same questions and who are facing up to their own violence.

This will also be a bit tricky.

Finding other men who will help you and support

you might be a bit like walking too close to the edge of a cliff.

It will be more beneficial if you can find a group that is offered by a counsellor or a counselling organisation that has a solid reputation in helping men to end their violence.

They have to be men who get it.

Often when men get together they can be a bit competitive.

They can avoid serious talk by joking around.

They might even let you off the hook by blaming your partner and excusing you for what you have done.

This will not help you to stay on the path.

They need to be men who truly hold a desire within them to be the best dads they can be, to be men who in their hearts put the safety and trust of their partner and their kids as number one.

You need to find men who will be honest with you.

They need to be men who truly respect women and don't put them down.

They need to be men who are also making changes in their own behaviour towards their partners.

They need to be men who are working on letting go of violence in any form, against any person.

They also need to be men who really understand the impact of the many types of controlling behaviours that men use.

These men will know how damaging controlling behaviours can be.

They will understand that it is not enough to stop using physical violence if other controlling behaviours continue; things like put downs, name calling, swearing, bossing, isolating.

I heard recently about a man who lost ten kilos in weight just by taking a photo on his phone of everything he ate and sending it to a couple of his friends.

Over time he changed what he ate and how much he ate.

He was being accountable to others for what he ate.

And this helped him change.

Being accountable to a few other men might help you to make the changes you want to make.

As long as they are all on the same page as you and don't let you swerve off track.

It may be difficult to find the right man or men to talk with honestly and openly.

Try contacting Relationships Australia.

For details of their services visit www.relationships.org.au.

Men might find it really difficult to speak truthfully about what they have done.

I have a suggestion for how you might be able to be really straightforward with another man and him with you.

You could do this with a small group of men too.

Ask each other if you are willing to answer three questions truthfully with each other.

Decide who will go first.

The person listening, simply listens to each answer.

When you have finished, he is like a mirror, repeating what he has heard you say.

One question at a time.

When you have answered all three questions, he can ask you if there is anything you want to add, anything you might have left out, or anything you may have given the wrong idea about.

Before you finish, is there anything you might have said that blamed or started to blame your partner for any of your actions?

Here are the three questions:

- Tell me about the first time that you used violence against your partner. Tell me what you did and what you said. (Remember this may have been putting her down, controlling her, punching a wall, slamming a door etc.).

- Now tell me about the last time that you used violence towards her.

- Finally, tell me what you think is the worst time that you used violence towards her.

These three questions can be quite helpful.

They will give you an idea of how long your partner has been hurt by you.

They will also give you an idea of how your use of violence has changed over time.

You might notice that your use of violence has become more frequent lately.

Or you might notice that it has changed and become harsher, causing more serious physical harm.

Or you might notice that at some point you stopped using physical violence but your verbal and emotional violence has increased.

And I wonder, how difficult would it be for you in this conversation to begin to talk with another man, or even in a group, about your sexual violence.

I wonder whether you would be able to face talking about this with another man and being honest about what the impact of this on your partner may have been.

Every time you meet together, ask each other whether you have remembered anything else that you want to add, or change anything that you said last time. This is a good way to be accountable to yourself and to each other.

Remember that this is not intended to shame you, it is meant to help you work out the things you want to stop doing.

You might feel some shame though. What will you do if you start to feel ashamed?

If you notice it, stop and say so. Take a breath or two and start again.

Remember that facing our shame about any of our actions is a part of becoming strong men.

And becoming a kind man, a strong man, will be so important in changing the future for our children.

THIRTY

Raising your sons to be kind men, strong men

So before we finish our conversation it is important that we talk a bit about raising our sons to be kind, strong men.

The truth is that they will learn the most about how to respect women from you, their dad.

If they see and hear your kindness towards their mother, they will learn to be kind.

If they know and trust that they are safe with you in their home, with their family, they will value safety.

If they hear you being respectful to women and girls, they will learn to respect them too.

If they hear you and your partner sharing decision making as equals, they will learn to value women too.

If they hear you genuinely acknowledging what you are unhappy with about your own actions, they will also learn to be honest with themselves.

If they know that you never choose to act violently towards anyone else, they will learn to make similar decisions.

You are their most important teacher.

You are the one who will show them how to live kindly towards others.

When you are driving and they are in the car, how will they see you treating other drivers?

When you are at a footy match together, what will they hear you call out at the other team?

What movies will you take them to see?

Or what computer games will you play together?

It is obvious that family patterns sometimes repeat through different generations in a family.

If you can see that there has been a pattern of violence in the generations of your family, will you be the dad who decides to break that cycle of violence?

Will you be the one who says "enough is enough"?

It may be the toughest thing you have ever done to sit down with your sons or your daughters and talk honestly with them about your violence and own up to your own actions.

It may be tough to admit to them that you were wrong in treating their mother the way you have.

You might feel vulnerable and weak, but this is when you will show them how strong you really are.

And when it comes to breaking the link between masculinity and violence, you are the one person who will give the strongest messages to your sons.

What will you teach them about how to play games and what sport is all about?

What will you teach them about competition and winning? Will it be a "win at all costs" message?

What will you teach them about how to deal with bullies?

What will you teach them about how to show affection?

Or how to share their emotions?

What will you teach them about how to relate sexually to others?

Will you use words like "sissy" or "poofter?"

Will you teach him to fight, or will you teach them non-violent ways to solve problems?

When you think about the kind of relationships you would like them to have in the future, what would they be like?

How can you help them to prepare for them?

What attitudes would you like them to develop towards women?

What will you teach them about being a kind and respectful partner?

What will you teach your sons about being kind men, strong men?

And I wonder about the hopes that you have for your daughters?

I am thinking about the way that you would like them to be treated by any men in their lives.

I am wondering if you want them to be treated fairly, kindly, safely.

How do you want your daughters to be treated sexually by men?

Do you want them to be the objects of men's abusive and disrespectful sexual jokes, comments or actions?

Do you want them to be in a relationship where they are not free to relate as equals, to share decision making, to be free to have their own friends and to make their own choices?

Do you want your daughters to live with the fear of being physically hurt if they do not do what their partner wants?

Do you want any future grandchildren to grow

up being frightened of being hurt by their dad or seeing their mum hurt by him?

These are really big questions to think about.

You are the one who can begin to change the future now.

THIRTY-ONE

Staying in touch

I would really love to hear from you if you wanted to tell me about the changes you are making and what is helping you to make these changes.

I have an email address below that you can use to write to me and tell me about what helped you to stop your violence.

I would also like to hear about how life as a dad is now different for you.

Anything at all that you want to tell me about the changes you have made, what has helped you and how your partner and kids now relate to you, would be really interesting to hear.

Perhaps this is a way of also helping other men to make similar changes.

Can you imagine hundreds, perhaps even thousands of men, deciding that they want to end their violence?

Can you imagine what a difference it would make to their partners and their kids if they were now living with the certainty of being safe in their own homes?

Can you imagine how our whole country would be different if thousands of men had the strength to face up to their violence and began to live with kindness in their families?

Can you imagine if one man ended his violence and then supported another man on a similar pathway?

This is the challenge before us all.

Whether we use violence or not, all of us as men can share this responsibility for standing up and speaking out to end men's violence against women.

If you have any questions or comments at all that you would like to share with me, I will do my best to answer you.

Tell me about the changes you are making.

Write to me at this email address:

kindmanstrongman@gmail.com

I have also suggested some places that will be able to guide you to find help in your local area or to find out more information.

Use these numbers to talk to a counsellor or to ask about finding a counsellor to support you in the changes you are making:

- MensLine Australia 1300 78 99 78 is a 24/7 counselling and referral service for men.

- 1800RESPECT 1800 737 732 is a national domestic violence counselling and referral service operating 24/7.

- White Ribbon Australia is a project that invites men to stand up and speak out against men's violence against women. Check out the website at www.whiteribbon.org.au.

- Our Watch is another helpful organisation with current information about ending your violence. Check out the website at www.ourwatch.org.au.

www.ingramcontent.com/pod-product-compliance
Lightning Source LLC
Chambersburg PA
CBHW071344080526
44587CB00017B/2964